A HUNDRED LITTLE 3D PICTURES

other books by the author

POETRY
Dawn Visions
Burnt Heart/Ode to the War Dead
This Body of Black Light Gone Through the Diamond
The Desert is the Only Way Out
The Chronicles of Akhira
The Blind Beekeeper
Mars & Beyond
Laughing Buddha Weeping Sufi
Salt Prayers
Ramadan Sonnets
Psalms for the Brokenhearted
I Imagine a Lion
Coattails of the Saint
Abdallah Jones and the Disappearing-Dust Caper (illustrated by the author)
Love is a Letter Burning in a High Wind
The Flame of Transformation Turns to Light
Underwater Galaxies
The Music Space
Cooked Oranges
Through Rose Colored Glasses
Like When You Wave at a Train and the Train Hoots Back at You
In the Realm of Neither
The Fire Eater's Lunchbreak
Millennial Prognostications
You Open a Door and it's a Starry Night
Where Death Goes
Shaking the Quicksilver Pool
The Perfect Orchestra
Sparrow on the Prophet's Tomb
A Maddening Disregard for the Passage of Time
Stretched Out on Amethysts
Invention of the Wheel
Sparks Off the Main Strike
Chants for the Beauty Feast
In Constant Incandescence
Holiday from the Perfect Crime
The Caged Bear Spies the Angel
The Puzzle
Ramadan is Burnished Sunlight
Ala-udeen & The Magic Lamp (illustrated by the author)
The Crown of Creation (illustrated by the author)
Blood Songs
Down at the Deep End (with drawings by the author)
Next Life
A Hundred Little 3D Pictures

THEATER / THE FLOATING LOTUS MAGIC OPERA COMPANY
The Walls Are Running Blood
Bliss Apocalypse

PROSE
Zen Rock Gardening
The Little Book of Zen

A HUNDRED LITTLE 3D PICTURES

POEMS

May 14, 1994 - September 11, 1995

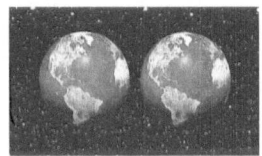

DANIEL ABDAL-HAYY MOORE

The Ecstatic Exchange
2013
Philadelphia

A Hundred Little 3D Pictures
Copyright © 2013 Daniel Abdal-Hayy Moore
All rights reserved.
Printed in the United States of America

For quotes any longer than those for critical articles and reviews, contact:
The Ecstatic Exchange,
6470 Morris Park Road, Philadelphia, PA 19151-2403
email: abdalhayy@danielmoorepoetry.com

First Edition
ISBN: 978-0-578-12560-2 (paper)
Published by *The Ecstatic Exchange,*
6470 Morris Park Road, Philadelphia, PA 19151-2403

Also available from *The Ecstatic Exchange:*
Knocking from Inside, poems by Tiel Aisha Ansari

TO SEE COVERS AND INSIDE PLANETS IN 3 DIMENSIONS, make the lines of sight of left and right eyes nearly parallel, as if looking at something far away. Then hold the image flat up against your face, slowly moving the image away without losing that focal point. The image will go blurry at first, but your eyes will fairly quickly lock into the stereogram's deeper (and uncanny) 3 dimensions on their own.

Cover collage by the author
Back cover author's photograph by Malika Moore

DEDICATION

To
Shaykh ibn al-Habib
(and the continuation of the Habibiyya)
Shaykh Bawa Muhaiyuddeen,
all shuyukh of instruction and ma'arifa
and
Baji Tayyaba Khanum
of the unsounded depths

*The earth is not bereft
of Light*

CONTENTS

Author's Introduction 10
The Field is a Fuzzy Conglomeration 13
Fist 14
The Joy of Composition 15
The Mummy 16
Stone 18
Wall of the Elements 19
New York, New York 21
The Little 3D Picture of Death 23
How Does Reality Come Through to Us? 25
Giant Dog 27
Between a Promise and a Taunt 29
Taking Shape 31
Parallel Rose 33
All the Books I Need 35
New Maple Tree 39
Saints Everywhere 41
Glass Skull 43
Twentieth Century Justice 45
Panga 47
The Sweet Grief of Loss 50
Death Bed 52
Leaves 58
Afraid of Mortality 59
Various Poems I Wanted to Write 62
Angels 64
Ocean City, New Jersey 71
Elaborations/Simplifications 74
The Journey 76

Top of the World, Bottom of the World   78
Borealis Sky   80
Sleep and Waking   82
Some Spiritual Secrets   84
A Bizarre Episode Concerning Stigmata   85
New Onset Atrial Fibrillation   87
Bookstore Coffee Shop   94
Death and Language   100
Alchemical Jewels   106
Six Couplets   107
The Conference of the Dead   109
I'm Awakened by Something   116
The Imager   118
The Sentence   123
Blue Scarf of Lights   127
God's Observation Window   129
Folk Poems   131
The Excavation   136
Continuum   141
The Process   144
Poem Written Out in the Coffee Bar   145
Every Poet is Foolish   149
Ah, That Unseizeable Moment   152
History Lesson   154
Are We Hugged by Angels?   157
Written During a Rainstorm   159
When I Pray   160
These Faces of Ours   163
Various Meetings with the Self   166
If You Worship a Goat's Head   168
The Naked Fishermen of Tinderzee   171

A Hundred People in a Room   174
Theft of a Coat   177
The Ballad of Rosalee   182
The Slow Wingbeat of Butterflies   184
Poem Written During the Interview by Charlie Rose
    of Robert McNamara April 19, 1995 in Which McNamara
    States That the Vietnam War Was Wrong   188
Preparations for Sleep   190
Everyone at the Mall   193
The Man with One Eye   194
The Oceans of Love   197
Palace in the Treetops   204
Ancient Ziggurat   205
Bad Stanzas   209
At Sea   212
Shake the Box   222
Aw, Go to Sleep   225
Cosmic Paradox   229
Doorknob   232
Seven Short Fables   234
A Very Short Poem   236
Eight Short Life Stories   237
Rawhide Figure   239
Silver Water from a Spout   242
A Place for the Night   244
Sweet Cosmologies   246
Poem on my 55th Birthday   252
Deals   254
Tissue Paper   256
Their Lips are Singing   257
Unforeseen Miracles   259

Sink or Swim   261
Paradox Lake   262
Terrain of the Heart   263
A Trillion Things   265
Train Wreck Reversed   268
The Land of Dreams   270
3D Pictures for Sale   272
Permission for Silence   274
Contentment's Garden   276
A Hundred Little 3D Pictures   279
Blue is an Excellent Color for Sky   282
Air   283

Index   286

AUTHOR'S INTRODUCTION

A Hundred Little 3D Pictures started out from those once-popular computer generated images a certain stare, unfocused or crosseyed, could render in layered three dimensions, with some really astonishing results. Some were enthralling, a mix of patterns and colors (the Japanese developing some very artistic results), others simply goofily decorative and far out. I think the first impulse after "hearing" the title in my usual way, taking it as a basis for the next period of inspiration (I can't completely explain how after finishing a book of poems, I begin a new one with a newly "received" title to work from, however loosely), was to just do imagistic descriptions of imagined 3D pictures, with some movement in the poems of depth and foreground, etc. But the poems kept getting bigger and bigger, no longer *little* 3D pictures but some in many parts and on a far wider canvas.

What happened, I think, was that imaginatively entering into this realm of 3D pictures, as it went along my focus became more dimensional, if such could be claimed. That by going or wanting to go in and in I found inspiration expanding rather than contracting. As time has gone on, I've found my poems coming with more concision, even occasional formality, rather than my usual practice of what has been called "open form." So it would seem ironic that when given the title of "A Hundred *Little* 3D Pictures" it would end up being the longest of my books to date (May of 2013).

Perhaps it's in line with the physics of the interior of an atom being, as it were, as large as the entire universe. It seems this is the way the world works, by Allah. That the Seen world is like a shell for the Unseen world, or vice-versa, and what is taken as real is illusion, and what is assumed to be more in the imaginal realm, is more reality. This gets us into a metaphysics of existence, on our journey, that as human beings, created by God in all His Mercy and in all our natural glory, reflecting His Glory, we are equipped and urged to forge into realms both seen and unseen, and in continuous gratitude to our Creator to find the domain and dimension of the Sacred that gives Light and meaning to our life. As a shaykh of Sufism has put it: "When you go into yourselves, you find the world; when you go out into the world, you find yourselves."

Recall the excitement in childhood when we looked into a diorama and saw back and back past whatever was being portrayed, not very far back really, perhaps, maybe only a shoebox length back, but peering through the front hole with the little flashlight or christmas bulb illuminating it, we saw a wee world that gave us shivers of delight. Or those Easter eggs with rabbity scenes in them, past a pastel filagreed and sugery porthole into an interior, mysterious world. Was this our first introduction into the world of contemplation, of inner journeying? Does the interest since then in holograms and these stereograms show us the parameters of consciousness greater than our daily one, that has within it, in fact, by Allah, the entire universe as well? As Allah ta'ala has said in hadith qudsi, *"The whole universe cannot contain Me, but the heart of the believer can contain Me."*

So, these little 3D pictures, for your viewing pleasure, along my route of poetry to, God willing, His Throne of Light, with my heartfelt blessings.

*Innamal kawnu ma'aanin
qaa'imaatun bis-suwar*
The reality of the universe is spiritual meanings
projected in the images of outward forms.

•

*Fa law 'arafa-l-insáanu qímata qalbihi
la anfaqa kulla-l-kulli min ghayri fitrati*
For if a person truly knew the worth of his heart,
he would give all he had without hesitation.

*Wa law adraka-l-insánu lidhdhati sirrihi
la qárina anfása-l-khurúji bi 'abrati*
And if a person came to know the bliss within his soul,
he would shed a tear of joy with every breath he took.

— *Sayyedina Shaykh Muhammad ibn al-Habib
(raheemullah)*

THE FIELD IS A FUZZY CONGLOMERATION

The field is a fuzzy conglomeration of
specks, splotches and
   textures of color the eye swims into from the
top then pulls back to see

sandstorm, each speck suspended in
   different horizontal planes as far back as the
eye can see to a
   sky that dissolves into
     cloudy depths,

and inside each speck the eye sees a cave that
also goes back in space, gritty belly-button of
dark and luminous color that seems to
extend back indefinitely, and there in the

exact middle of each belly-button
a tiny dragon of fiery power
lifts its head in a

corolla of flames and
flashes its eyes.

5/14

FIST

A city street, back from the
  foreground in parallel lines that
converge as they extend back, San Francisco
    Victorian-type houses on either side, gloom-gray
with little black outlines around the windows,

then in the horizon line sky
a burst of golden brilliance, sunrise or sunset
blindingly bright, the eye
focuses for a minute then

out of the brightness a large human fist
lunges forward, but when the
eye rests more deeply into its focus

the fist is a chariot pulled by golden horses, manes
gleaming back, handsome toga'd youth
with pure countenance holding the white reins and
urging the golden chariot forward.

5/14

THE JOY OF COMPOSITION

Ah, the astonishing joy of composition, those
   fuzzy meteors humming their way forward out of a
     deep background of interior space
from black purple to rosy gold
becoming words which float into place and
worlds which open their locked arbor doors to display
gardens of close-clipped hedge and heavenly geometry,
esplanades of hexagons dropping away back into
   flat expanses with paths between vertical
     cypress, shadows and lights carving
pathways as well between
the edges of this world of second-hand smoke and
    first-hand fear

and its sister world cupped so closely and invisibly
     into this one where
all fears are dissolved away in a
real golden chalice that's lifted from an icy pool
with billows of steam rolling down its
sides to spell out
   sweet sentences of
long life, delicious repose, and the
    wisdom that comes of

     ultimate surrender.

5/16

THE MUMMY

They excavated the mummy who'd been dead
millenniums and he
   must've been a saint since his
     flesh was fresh, his glassy eyes
       intact, a smile on his
         lips, his delicate hands
over his heart, and when they endeavored to pull his
   hands away there glowed in the place on his
     breastbone under them
a metropolis of birds making rippling
     ribbons of flight between tall pillars with so
   silvery a sunlight radiating its venetian blind
     rays slantwise that it nearly
blinded their eyes, their
  oh so worldly eyes, and a blue
     water gushed out, Nile lily pads
floating on the froth-waves like elf-boats, dragonflies
   hovering like helicopters above them.

It was a
strategy of heaven to invade our
usual notions, and the onrush of heron's cries and
rattling of reeds in their reed beds and the
spokes as of bicycle wheels of light
fluttering past and clattering in an
   uprush from that mummy's living
     place of refuge and saintly
aggression into the mundane of our world without

ritual or recognition —
he smiled almost,
he almost cocked an eye.
His thin index-fingers made a peaked arch,
 perched together so many centuries

on that single
watch.

5/16

STONE

A golden stone that floats forward on a
    slender jet of water, so
slender you wonder how it could support the
    stone's weight, turning it
slowly in the mushroom cushion at the
top of the jet, the upshooting
strands of water not intertwining but
rising individually from some
unseen source below the
foreground,

the stone
tilts, we move in to
take a deeper look at it (as we can
  do here, "deeper," not just "better"), and we
do look into that golden stone, a
dome opens up in mental image behind our
eyes big enough not only for the
suspended stone to appear in, but for the
stone to both surround that
dome of space and be
surrounded by it simultaneously, transforming

our beings into the poised beak of a golden bird
standing in the dome on
    slender legs,

fishing in the black pond at our feet
for light.

                                                5/16

WALL OF THE ELEMENTS

Bricklayers in a trance from
Tibet laying
   minutely carved
gold bricks in mystic equilibrium with the
proper mantras and blessings from the highest bishop
could not
have created a wall more perfect than this
exquisite inlay of glass and
   diamond,
wall of the elements, squares of
water, fire, air and earth in frozen
   miniature
that look like
any minute they might burst out and
create real havoc with some previously
     unruffled pedestrian,

there is an area of controlled whirlpool, objects
   in stasis in a giant watery corkscrew of light
     sitting above a
        bottomless abyss,

there is fire like ignited green velvet
burning its hairs in mile-high conflagration
through which you can see
   an infinitely stepped kingdom of burnished sand
     erected like the dream of a
demon on a desert in Hell,

or the area of air, boundless, gloriously bursting
    light in tetrahedronic spaciousness, geometric
figures of triangular complexity turning as slow as
the growth of mouse-teeth set in tumblers of glass
   one inside the other, each showing a
     face of The Void to the
        galaxy of strangeness and silence that
   surrounds it,

and on the earth plot in this rare wall
(better imagined by beetles than I can)
  which seems erected between
ourselves and absolute chaos (a
momentary illusion of material reality shot up
    between death
and the spinning tops of The Divine Presence,
embraceable cyclones of
    serene benevolence),
there are plotted puzzle-shapes of crystalline meadows
and slow streams of crushed stone running
   through them with a
    falcon's shadow speeding across their
  slopes

as the falcon of vigilant completion flies across the earth
and disappears past an edge that is
simultaneously out the
corners of our eyes

shimmering in
midnight's dark.

NEW YORK, NEW YORK

for Michael Lorimer

I'm actually sitting at one of those
glassed-in New York restaurants that
jut out into the sidewalk, watching the
people go by, and the
little 3D picture here would be

in everyone's heart simultaneously, in the
gimpy old guy with grizzled chin, the
   Chinese waiter rushing by in apron and black shoes, the
man with umbrella holding his cleaning in its plastic bag,
the overwrought mother with her three overactive children,
the lovely secretive girl in green slacks, the
black brother with his baseball cap backwards and
     black glasses,

the little 3D picture here
would burst like a blooming of once-a-year roses,
and it too would have dark reddish-purple deep richness
   inside the base, and grow
delicately peach near the outer edge, and peering way in we'd see
a gathering of lions under green leaves licking their
   paws, and a white egret
sitting on a post about to fly, and it would suddenly
fly forward with beauteous wings
   just flicking the edge of the picture on
either side,

and at its closest point to our own faces its
feathery face would show sphinx-like ageless quietude,
    high cheeks, slitted eyes, a
        sweet aroma

fills the air, golden
light filters down from the sides onto a
flat mirror placed

   symmetrically
   under a black sky.

                                                      5/19

THE LITTLE 3D PICTURE OF DEATH

for Kamala Cesar

Then there's the little 3D picture of death:
   a skull pops out of the page.
(I write this in a penthouse in the shadow of the
   Empire State Building) —
The eye is afraid to look, but the skull
doesn't wink or grin, it's just an
   object in space, it offers

nothing from its side to scare us, it's the fact that we
touch our own face and feel the skull underneath,
we carry death's porcelain mausoleum within us. That
hard white mobile like a
   monogram from space of our own
elsewhereness when we're gone, leaving those
bony utensils that supported us all these years
like museum artifacts good only for
   carbon dating and
      stop-frame horror movies and to know that

some perfectly pliable and sweet-natured
creature rode around on those bones in life,
leaving them behind for recycling, arranged in their
perfect assemblage underground —

the ground sifts open into a deep
rectangle in space, those gloriously sculpted

bones with their delicate phalanges and
   foot-bones float in the air against a
disappearing blue background,
clouds of magenta and green slowly pass in the
distance, an oboe note is sounded, a
fingertap dry on a tom-tom,

the bones come forward and
slip into our persons unaware

and we sit straight, smile, blink eyes,
brush back our hair.

                                                     5/20

HOW DOES REALITY COME THROUGH TO US?

How does Reality come through to us?
If we're always
   missing the boat, or taking the word of
     someone who doesn't know,

how can we be sure to do anything, to act with the
confidence of a saintly wanderer with white
   parrot on his shoulders who with
staff and bowl always is in the
right place at the right time with a
    smile on his face and a
      good word? To be

in sync, on target, with what is
decreed bubbling away happily on our
front burner. *Ah!*

I arrived at the prayer while they were
rolling up the paper they'd unrolled on the
ground in a city tennis court
   for people to pray on. I'd taken the
word of a New York Muslim car mechanic who told me
of a mosque around the corner from where I was staying.
I wanted to go to the 'Eid Prayer next morning. But next morning the
mosque was closed. I inquired and
   found out they were
praying at the big mosque two subway stops away
and about ten blocks of walking.

Finally, an hour later, when I arrived at the
right place, the convergence of
   two avenues, they were
rolling up the paper they'd laid out, droves of men in
    white robes walking home along the
      sidewalk, women in colorful shawls, the prayer was
over. Reality had other ideas than
   what I thought should be.

Christopher Columbus lost in the middle of the sea,
improvised. He was way
  off when he got to his destination,
     and right on. Now I'm
sitting on a
park bench in Manhattan watching
Pakistani Muslims roll up huge lengths of butcher paper
in a country that began from a
   massive miscalculation, whose
"discoverer" (though he can hardly be
    credited with discovering somewhere so
lengthily and deeply inhabited)
never knew it wasn't where he thought it was,
        died deluded!

We're all here from that delusion.
Constantly bewildered,
the bursting
bubbles of our hearts

afloat in the open sea!

5/21

GIANT DOG

Having a giant dog
(almost as big as
   the house), on a
leash extends half the length of
the world, wearing bright
lipstick (bright green, bright orange)
and standing under a
   waterfall of
air, air cascading over
rocks, holding the leash of the
giant dog to catch the
twilight's light, smiling hard.

This was all of existence to that
youth, this was all existence
that youth knew.
Piano music did not distract,
nor night terrorize. For the

giant dog was its heart
so vast youth could travel for days without
hitting shore, and the
leash was its lifetime
     so long no
visible end was in sight, youth
    held on to one end
        and was glad.

This itself is a
3D picture, decked out in
velvet. Prickly with

cactus points where
least expected.

5/27

BETWEEN A PROMISE AND A TAUNT

Don't you get the feeling in this
   world of three dimensions that
everything lies somewhere between a
promise and a taunt, an obstacle and a
    bridge to dimensions far more
glorious and fluid than these three or even
four, not that these experiential ones are

inside out to more real ones exactly, but that
all the joys and annoyances, all the
glitter that is gold and even the
ground under our feet is not
either permanent or even the best
possible of all worlds,

that it's a funnel or tunnel to the
world where these dimensions we
enjoy and savor are a bit like
glisten on a sweaty body, foam on the
   tops of waves, a barely glimpsed
      movement in the
bottom of a deep pool, and that the

place where we apprehend dimension, that
place in heart and mind combined which
pushes aside at the last minute to reveal
a crystal staircase, an amber spiral, a
whirlwind of slow-motion water, that

lifts us and opens us out, where the tallest
Himalayas here are specks poking through low-lying
   mist, the great oceans are
     tears in the corner of
       a compassionate eye,

that we are greeted and welcomed there
where we were mistreated or misunderstood here,
each of us, no one more than another,

that that place, now unknown to us,
is the perfect dimension of

complete contentment.

                                            5/30

TAKING SHAPE

You've got to be astonished at how
   a figure takes shape out of a
     landscape, coming right toward you,
it might be a lover, it
might be a stag with dynamite antlers to
   blow your toothpick metropolis away,

a figure we've longed for, eyes ablaze with
affirmation of the sweet liberty of life
we've never affirmed enough, we always
   feel a gulf, but
here he is, face shining,
framed out of a conjunction of trees and hills, sky and
   the sounds coming out of the earth at
midday, tangled with bird-squeezle and dorp,
   tweedle and trill of those
sky-level fliers,

out of the dazzle and roughage of molecular matter
a person, not quite a person, we
   might think "angelic," black eyelashes and
   pink tongue,

come forward out on the air
presenting us with the passionate breath of the
next world in exchange for the
melting skeleton of this, this world putting its
weave of words and rocks and

   winds together to form a
mesh background for this eye-popping
      blaze of light to

stand forth!

PARALLEL ROSE

for Ira Cohen

I would squander a lifetime's visions for an
   encapsulated squint at the Source that would
change the course of events for me as well as
for Mr. Harringbone's prize rooster, one
gaze enough to rearrange the molecular
    structure of all being, living and inert,

in one ray of light so vast you'd see
whole Niles of flotillas carrying all the
great and terrible Pharaohs to their flood, all the
divine redeemers and geniuses of ontology,
every backroom physicist with red alembic and
   nitrate powder mixed in
     honey and owl's breath

would also celebrate the triumphal entrance under
arches of eyebrows of
the angelic legions of another kind of matter
   altogether, white lions in
vanishing parallel rows raising their
   heads simultaneously to roar a
     greeting to the
        farthest stars!

And what a reply we'd get from deep space!
Bleeps gone to spherical symphonies so slow it makes

    Bruckner sound like ragtime, but with
        never a dull moment. The
End of the Universe in a bugle-note. All
oceans rolled up and continents folded,
arm over arm over arm, until the
      chain of being becomes
          human again. Light out of

all eyes at once! Nothing to
    salvage. All our
notes and all our
papers in order. I have ten

billion more poems to
write before I die, what about
      you? I tip the
eagle of my hat to you, and dip its brim in
amethyst blood left when the
troops of angels who begin things anew

dragged their
wings as they passed through

writing this one.

                                            6/9

ALL THE BOOKS I NEED

I think I've got all the books I need now
to rebuild the world,

one on bridge-building to lay out
cities and thoroughfares, spidery
   girders made of silkworm thread
      stronger than iron,
one on architectural masterpieces to construct
magnificent domed meeting-places, houses for
the consummation of nuptials,
    elaborate bee-hives of quartz crystal and
       spun glass,

grand
esplanades winding out from
dazzling building to building, landscaped with giant
neon-red cockscombs and birds of paradise
   gleaming golden and satiny in the sun, sunflowers
"counting the steps of the sun," their
     straggly heads big as billboards,
jade-colored lawns sloping everywhere, rippling along like the
   elusive back of the Loch Ness monster,
disappearing into little woods and copses
where picnickers frolic as they
   laugh their way into the dark between
      fir trees to find
spots to spread tablecloths cut in the
    shapes of mammoth moth-wings, bluer

than the blue of Morpho butterflies,

cypresses on horizon hilltops to express the vertical,
   (spindly black flames licking white sky),
channels of ice-water descending everywhere as in the
   Alhambra in Granada, culminating in

innumerable fountains, the lovely white noise of
incessant water for bathing and
   splashing on the
hot faces of this new earth's inhabitants,

I've got books for all this,
and I've got books of velveteen
instruction, hypotherms of knowledges so
simple they're abstruse, silvery as the
   water gushing from those
     fountains, high jets of fine spray through which
lithe cougars leap from time to time, and
lions smelling of dark musk and
sheer animality, yawning a roar that could
   collapse the creation and
     recreate it from
scratch again in minute detail in the
   gleam of their leonine eye-teeth bared in the
     moonlight,

white tigers also from time to time leaping through with
bright agate eyes, ibex and
gazelle making their
fashionable appearance,

then there are street lamps hammered from
nuclear transcendence glittering on each side of
every road possible, I've got
the *"Book of Lights"* too, and diagrams even
   the most distracted and engrossed in
      material hungers can
assemble themselves with a
long afternoon or two in front of them and
      a pure intention,

then there's the book of transportation,
monorails, bullet-sped, faster-than-light,
winding around impossible mountains of
   unrecyclable detritus calcified from earlier
      cultures,
I've got that book somewhere, and the one that
   renders civilization's waste harmless, carving it into
      haunted parapets and
   monuments to planet-suicide redeemed,

and doorways! I've got a
hinged book on doorways, describing some so
   small you have to get on your hands and knees to
      look through them, like Alice,
sub-molecular, intercellular, as well as
some bigger than the state of Delaware,
and one horizontal door that opens onto
B-movie terror so acidic and joy so
   carbohydrolic that shiny flying fish leap
      from the black surface of the water below them
to cut a clean slice back into the

darkness again just as the door closes
over them.

Ah, Utopias are so fragile!
Fascists always want to take them over because of their
   idealized innocence,
or fantasists with important
     degrees and titles who posit we've all
        descended from apes
when it's actually the other way around, men into apes
   miserably slinking away, tails curved around
       noses,
our stereoptic eyesight proof enough not only of
our immediate Divine Origin, but the
continuing presence of Divine Activity
with every breath we take, every glance we make,

and there are books for that too,
books which show how all the Divine Light's
mosaic pieces fit together
side by side by angular side to make a
magnificent metropolis everyone but
   Moctezuma'd feel comfortable in
    (no ritualized shedding of blood),

and which I lie back down now
to observe, command
   construction and
watch go up
in my sleep.

                                                  6/17

NEW MAPLE TREE

Eight billion "little people," not
    leprechauns or pygmies, not
figments of hallucinatory conjured-up
Art visions out of the burnt sepias of
Bruegel or Bosch, not
tiny intelligences from planetary paranoias of
   Sci-Fi writers on Benzedrine, nor
big-headed inhabitants of Lilliput, not the
microscopic antics of greenish fairy tales nor
the delirium tremens stupors of once genius playwrights
        frightened at walls,

not acrobatic lice on the backs of subaqueous hairy beasts
nor mind-tricks deep in the brain, sparks from
   lobe to lobe filled with
minutest information in high-definition detail,
    subway maps of
heights Empyrean and
lower depths hellish, Dantesque
roustabout Satans yelling at sinners, nor
scintillant wing-spangles from beyond
     Jupiterian outreaches,

no, none of these,
but grand magistrates in ermine robes and powdered wigs
at high desks passing judgment on gnarled criminals with
howling childhoods,
kings and queens in satin pumps and lambsdown underwear

conjugating the multitude permutations of
royal prerogative while seated on Baroque thrones made of
moose horn and human thigh bones,
dazzling troubadours and Mongolian jugglers with
    bear-grease for hair tonic
and millions of housewives over desperation dishwashers
and millions of husbands tangled in corporate neck-braces
all so tiny they could fit on the head of a pin you can
stick in your lapel as you
whistle down the lane,

and yet this is all of us, cleverer and
   bigger than anyone else, richer or
      poorer, fuller or
 hungrier than
        anyone,
smarter or dumber, cuter or
    uglier, all
more microscopic in reality than the
shadow cast by a tiny hair growing on the
bacillus of a gnat's eyebrow,

and that's why I'm
happy sitting by my new four foot tall maple tree just
transplanted into my row house back garden in Philadelphia
hoping its roots will take and its
   trunk prosper,
bathing in the glance of God
as a cricket might bathe in

raindrops sliding off a plant leaf.

SAINTS EVERYWHERE

"Don't call me a saint"
— Dorothy Day

There are saints everywhere, saints in their
   beds aloft in the ship of night
whose dreams are breathless marathons passing
     significant heavens up ring after ring
to the highest center
   encircled by a filigree of angels.

There are gaunt saints under trees holding leafy staves
whose gazes are neither focused on
the outside nor
    inside worlds, they
      stand aloft on long bamboo legs
       and watch herons of blue light
take off and land among shadows with
    faces of sick children.

There are saints calling intercontinental long distance
who leave prayers on our message machines
to enlighten the universe about the
bounty bestowed on each one of us from the single
Divine Source of creation, whose strong voices grow
    frail by the thunderous
bulk of their message and whose
eyes are so blue the whole sky
    becomes their apprentice in blueness,

unknown saints, known or unknown to themselves or others,
whose neon brightness in their bones lights up
   a corner in
heaven somewhere known or unbeknownst to them,

car mechanic saints greasy and creased under cars,
faces like winter street lamps through catastrophe ice storm,

grocery clerk saints no more than seventeen years old
tote loaded bags to the trunk, help the
   invalid in, Boy Scout stuff that in
     this world's like
       orchids in the arctic of our
universal social breakdown,

saints with faces of butterfly powderiness,
saints with faces of blasted wood, broken iron,
whose hearts are valleys with
openings all the way to the sea,
whose feet are always
taking them places, and whose
hands are always doing things,

whose thoughts and whose
heartbeats have enough
electricity in them to run
one or two New Yorks and a few scattered

Cairos through the most
difficult seasons.

                                           7/10

GLASS SKULL

He wakes up to find
   his skull has turned to glass.
He sees prisms through the eyeholes.
Everything is outlined in blazing rainbows.
He blinks and vistas extend in all directions,
he closes his eyes and they shoot forward even more.

His skull is a thick
   primordial glass, paperweight
     rounded, polished like
agate, but he doesn't panic. The
faces that greet his see no anomaly and still
smile, the
days proceed as usual, birds
sing and stop their song.

But everywhere he looks, fine combed electrical
rainbows run like wiring around everything,
turning pages become glorious
   tunnel affairs, petting the
sleek black cat of his childhood becomes a
     mythic revisiting, those
yellow-green eyes looking straight at him
inside a wavy engineering of prismatic intertwined
      outlines with
blackness, the meow itself
waking up in his dormant bones
echoes off Magellanic plains, cave resonances

from earlier eras. Flicker-light
that tell stories and visual
outlines that hold the
   coded messages of pre-history.

One blink and he is there among tall pampas grass
with a sinew slingshot. Another blink
and he's sailing with Drake, rounding
   San Francisco Bay in broad daylight.

Such you can do with a glass skull.

His eyes become hot marbles.

His life having switched on
a light in another room than the one
he normally dwells in.

And the light in that room
perpetually shifting.

7/13

TWENTIETH CENTURY JUSTICE

It's a dialogue in private between
the accused and his attorney in which
the attorney hopes to get him off on a
technicality, the accused having
set fire to an arena and all its
bleachers, in which
twenty thousand people perished, and
those who survived were mowed down by
machine-gun fire out of blimps and
   helicopters, he having
taken the mayor's daughter hostage and
doing what he did with her, because of
deep-seated psychological problems, it's
   all very clear in the
     ratchety chronology of his
      tattered life no
   homeless maniac on speed could ever
       hope for, but in this

behind-bars dialogue they hatch a
foolproof defense based on the fact that
when the police apprehended him in the
motel, having
   kicked in the door without a warrant, etc., and
then handcuffed him to an
electric pole where naked wires were
     dangling, etc., and right in a
      bed of poison ivy, etc., out on the

busy highway where he was
trying to outrun a falange of twenty police cars, etc.,

and they do it! They get him off, his genius
attorney, *the accused walks free!*
Lives on for years in
sumptuous hotel rooms.

But one early morning
when he's about to die, a strange figure in
full armor blams through his deathbed wall
  as if it were cellophane
and opens his visor and
flames shoot out of his eyes and sparks flash
    out the
      tips of his fingers, and
although the accused eluded
human justice by a legal technicality in
this world,

at the last minute this
charred furnace on blazing legs with
goggly eyes of white-hot ingots
opens his mouth like a fiery drop-chute and
with an infernal echo shouts:

"You!
Come with me."

7/17

PANGA

> "Throughout the country, the panga was the murder weapon of choice... A full panga job took about twenty minutes. First the hands were chopped off, then deep gashes were scored in the back, and finally the head was whacked. If you preferred a quick death, by a bullet, you had to pay for it. The going rate was five thousand Rwandan francs, or about thirty-five dollars."
> — Flight from Death,
>   by Alex Shoumatoff (The New Yorker)

What about goblins tearing out my entrails,
glass ships cutting through my body with
   haunted sea-captains lashed to the mast,
army ants big as bolognas, or
lifted high in an elephant's trunk and
   thrown down onto freshly cut bamboo spikes!

Tied to a Nile barge to be nibbled on by crocodiles?
Thrown down a volcano's jaws — O let me be

 virgin again! Let me be
grasped by the mythical Roc bird's claws and
dropped down a canyon of obsidian heated to a
   boiling frenzy, or
tie me to tracks and let the
  Midnight Express and the
   Orient Express crash across me to do their
steam-driven Cuisinart on my organically grown parts!

Lower me down a mine-shaft in a basket and
fill the mine with laughing gas, or
let me run with hilarious hyenas on all fours until I drop,
or cook me in a pie fit for a king, I'll
   sing for my supper!

I'll pray for a long cloak of light to wrap me in its
loving squeeze — though I
  don't deserve it, the
    cloak of light promised to martyrs, those whose
     feet have stepped on
    fugitive blue feathers from
 yesteryear's angel-wings, haphazardly
   floated to earth,
placed there by Absolute Destiny to be stepped on,
since there are no accidents in the universe,

and we wake up from this life with our
eyes wide open and our
hearts full of birdsong!

So, do what you will, cut me in pieces, take the
thirty-five dollars as payment for the
next guy who can't
  afford such luxury (a quick
   silver ticket to a
long, slow Paradise).

Let my smile be your sole payment as my
eyes cloud over in this life like
blinds drawn down in a

cheap hotel room with dark wallpaper and stained mattress

to open on vistas your brutality can't fathom,
and the swing of your panga, warrior,
can't resonate

as its blade hits bone in the
bitter science of your lacklove forlorn.

7/20

THE SWEET GRIEF OF LOSS

If I could write any poem at all
I'd put it up on some
   peak at an almost
     oxygenless height surrounded by a
pewter-like glitter so clear and bright,
a stainless steel blue sky, white
slopes and whiter
peaks, cloudless, air so
   light each breath lifts you
     higher, and then

out of the pure sky a doorway, time
   shatters, like icicles at each
     side of our sight you can hear
the chimes of timelessness snowing horizontally
     at each end of space, and this

door suddenly breathes as well, takes in a
breath, we enter it unquestioningly, we take
zebra-stripe steps across very
   wide gulfs, down straight shafts of
     chasms we can see
turquoise water, frothing rapids, tops of
cities, passing clouds,

we step, we go up, we make that
leap that waits for the
   biological body to catch up,

there the great bison herd of the sun waits for
morning light to nourish it, there
a panoramic sweep of Native America across its
settlements and migrations, and looking down
we can also see
those domed metropoli of the future glinting back
with pearlescent oil-and water metallic colors
flashing in the depths there

as we continue our
   atmospheric climb up steps no one can
     actually even visualize, they're
supported by repeated prayers whispered at dawn,
their pillars that reach from
   earth-curve to heaven's concave
are the sweet grief of loss we've felt from the
first death to now, and those
pillars are strong,

the climb is short, but the
depth of it gouged into our
hearts by its light is
long.

7/27

DEATH BED

It seems that
  people die in their beds when
    no one's in the room — we wait for a
break in the social chord so we can be
totally alone with it, give ourselves
    totally up to it, and when
someone comes back to see us, we're gone, eyes
half open but clicked forever into place unseeing,
never to look upon anyone again, never to
     cross eyebeams or flood with
       tenderness,
but like an outdoor movie theater after
closing time, giant empty
screen in the dark, speakers sticking up at
      orderly intervals,
silent —

but maybe what happened while we were out
leaving the dying person alone for a moment
was really a riot of frenzied
processions, brass bands and
runaway locomotives of event come to
claim the simple dying person with the
greatest of dramatic flourishes — skies and walls of
ice and fire open up,
raging blue lions come galloping forward,
their mouths open onto illuminated mirrors in which we
    see ourselves not as

dying but as being born —

and behind the lions are The Temptations,
glorious Rockette-like choruses, plumed and spangled,
ready and willing to barter the things of this
   world for a song, for a flicker of
recognition from us at the last that we
want this world to go on forever with us in it —
they sing and tell jokes, they tempt us with
     mansions made of diamonds,
        limousines made of glass, hilltop fortresses at
          dawn on faraway islands surrounded by
lukewarm tropical waters, mountainous vistas of
  a this-worldly peace well protected and
      heavily armed, but we're

already floating midway between
this world and the next and not so
easily fooled — we pass on it, they

     evaporate.

Song echoes long along corridors like
natural canyons as we
open out onto desert extravaganzas —
then comes a march in slow elegant strides of the great
populace of wisdom-holders, proffering the
sacred mask illumined from within by a
sacred light, and they each have their personal

emblematic animal, gryphons, St. Jerome's lion,

hippogryphs, bird-like statuesque familiars,
each of their faces wrinkled with joy to see us on our
death beds, each hand held out with a
lapis lazuli scroll containing a formula that
only needs one glance from us to be brought to
life, as our glance leaves this
   life, leaps the bridge of
      space in an arc of
half-lidded joy, and these
spectral Knights of Pity and Sweet Compassion take us by our
      hand

which if
seen in the death-room in which we lie
would look like a passing
flutter of energy in the wrist, a
   flitting pulse in the
      fingers.

Then fiery horsemen on black
horses appear: "Ready? Leave
   everything behind, the

childhood house with all its memory crannies of
kitchen smells, wallpaper smells, deep down basement smells
(our childhood house appears majestically out of the
   floor in a geyser of golden
      flood),

leave it all behind, and all those
long summers of youth and too-rapid

summers of old age, leave them all behind! The
   later kisses and pressings of
body against body as if at the
bottom of an ocean, or out in
   space floating weightless, and then

as if on a screen skyscraper-high all those
bodies in naked resplendence appear with giant
faces transformed from desire to
   angelic flesh-purity, feathery, glistening,
     soapy, looming, whispering back all the

love-words you spoke but set more deeply in their
true celestial contexts, flickers of
   neon crackling around each
syllable, hovering over an
   abyss of light
   they slowly sink into.

The dying person is taking advantage of a few
seconds of being alone in the room when
Blam! The sky opens up like the Red Sea and
a massive celebration of millions of joyous
souls appears on a bright golden mountainside
   with turquoise and silver
sky just above it, the roof of it,
     angel wings like palm trees
arching high-waving fronds together as they
knit their tips into a
     dome of concave radiance.

The Death Angel, rainbow-faced,
our true spiritual double, comes straight out of the
   light for us, walks right
up and puts his
face into ours to the sound of surf against
   cliffs, volcanic rollings,
Jupiterian swivels in outer space — and there's a
heave from under our backs, there's a
bridge that appears horizontal to our
horizontal feet and we're
   already walking —

the procession is shadowless, deep as an
African afternoon,
faces all on a mission,
still and serene,
   determined and en route to
a higher elevation by way of
the unravelling of our carefully woven
   personalities into their
     delicate constituents, letting the
tangle lie in a heap
  unusable evermore,

each sweet vein of us infused now with a greater liquid,
each sweet heartbeat soft now like drum taps on a
late afternoon battlefield resonating out
   in a greater radius,

each hesitation of limb or
  uncertainty of bodily conviction

made and measured into a single form,
which takes leave of its physical casing

and walks along behind its
starry guide pouring out into the Next World,
a giant whip-snap of light in the air at the
brightly lit head of the procession!

I wait for them all to leave before I
also leave, singing my heart out in
    glorious courage facing the
Next World perspirationless, breathless,
singing suddenly and victoriously
   at the top of my voice
      absorbed into the
singing abounding everywhere around me —

when relatives and loved ones come back into the room

there's no one there dying anymore,

there's no one at all there anymore —

gone.

                                                 7/29

LEAVES

There's an infinite leafiness of leaves in these
   breeze-blown trees, green
     featheriness in tiny incremental
       ascending leafy stairways to the very
sunlit tops of these trees,

shelves of green leaves pouring jagged-edged
   waterfalls of green water-like leaves wavering
     down, dark
undershadows under domed leafy crowns, deep 3D deeps that
   extend back into distant
3-dimensional backdrops of trees, trunks and sunlight
   alternating, sunlight and
trunks, trunks and sunlight —

all to incessantly sibilant
cicada accompaniment chittering high up there
in those incessantly fluttering green

leaves.

                                                                     8/3

AFRAID OF MORTALITY

Anyone afraid for his mortality
as a square wheel of green jello and hawk skeletons
   rolls over his prone body,

anyone frightened of his own shark-nosed shadow against the
wall of a paper lantern whose fragile sides
are his body, his house, his whole life
about to catch fire and fly up like an idea dissolving
   into the darkness of mind as well as the
pitch delirium of night,
whose hide is not as thick as a zoo rhinoceros
lolling back and forth on its
puppy-dog feet rather than
blindly running down a gazelle whose
actual fright of rippled muscle and shivering skin
is more like a sea creature able to
   dart under a scallop shell amidst a
      jet spray of bubbles —

but here are no bubbles, no
   jet spray, only
stick-to-itiveness
and a funny body-shaped door which one day
one of us is going to have to check out,
and one by one all of us are going to
have to go through, one at a time — and the
order is important, crucial, but goes
so far back in time before they even

jackknifed the poor body, bound its back and
knees-up'd legs together and lowered it into a
narrow pit with celestial
   travel gear, water jug, bartering nuggets of
     jewelry, food inedible millenniums
       later, but nutritious nonetheless —

if anyone is afraid of getting washed up, of
his or her star getting eclipsed by better,
   younger, cuter, smarter, more insanely
clever than any of us in our zaniest
vest and baggy slinkies (pat. pending),
all these thoughts in outboard sput-spurts clouding our
usually crystal-clear mirror as we
line up what we say with what we do,
   or what we did with
     what we will say,

like adolescents down at Police Headquarters for
vandalizing a house under construction by
throwing a few bricks into a ditch,
afraid for the record that will get
started on our behalf and
   held up illuminated in front of a
backdrop of distant nebulae and star-shaped
seahorses outlined in
   pale lavender.

There is truly nothing in heaven and earth
that can stop compliments from hitting the
   ears of beauty,

or the bitterly sarcastic comments from reaching
the misshapen and huge donkey ears of
   ugly despair, that
stares into a nosedive of
     thought debris and rhythmless heartbeats
and many-story deep abyss of throwing oneself
down it belly up and about to
break our backs into a multi-dozen of
   newly minted pairs of dice
100% of which are going to
come up zero, guaranteed!

Anyone afraid of any of this, should find a
good deal on alligator shoes, the
    real things, and go
  wading into the Everglades in search of
     his lost childhood,
or clap two woodblocks together in the
   strictest monastery in Kyoto,
or sing close Mongolian harmony with
oneself in the smokey reality of
a Joe's Bar & Grill right near the
train station, with the
   freight train on time again after
     forty-some-odd years
  and the millionaire aunt with
     fingertip diamonds on all ten
waving from the door before disembarking,
we never ever seeing her face,
but bathe in the mythical midnight
    radiance of her glow!

                                          8/4

VARIOUS POEMS I WANTED TO WRITE

I wanted to write a nature poem
but an owl stole my fountain pen and a
rabid skunk drank my ink.

I wanted to write a war epic
but a hole broke through the hold of the sub and I
   sank, *all hands on deck* —

I wanted to write a love poem but love
was a burning bicycle careening downhill —

I wanted to write a surreal poem
but the everyday light of the kitchenette I
   sit in to write sucked up all imaginative
     juxtapositions and leaps of the
       unconscious into a
   few squares of perfectly fitted masonite —

I wanted a write a dream poem
but the Loch Ness Monster I spotted in the
   middle of Dream Lake turned out to be
    my senile grammar school principal
summoning me to her office —

I wanted to write a comic poem
but someone had substituted identical ball-bearings
for my typewriter keys, and white-out was
cleaning fluid leaving huge widening spots on my tie —

I wanted to write a history of mankind
but man was not kind and is still
   seeking kindness in all the
      wrong places —

I wanted to write a sonnet but
   sound wore a bonnet and got caught in
     a net of the sun and then
       sat on it —

I wanted to write a poem about life
and a hundred suspension bridges leapt into
   place like those movies of bridges getting
      blown up that are run backwards so that
a bridge miraculously reconstitutes itself out of its
own smoke and rubble, making a
   perfectly crossable bridge —

I wanted to write a poem about death,
its abrupt exits
and glorious entrances

but I died.

                                                   8/4

ANGELS

1

They revolve around the earth in constant
    revolution and counter-revolution,
contrary currents combing through each other
above the earth's rotation, angelic
    sheath around the physical globe,

layer infinitely more subtle and infinitely
tougher than the visible ozone layer,
glitter of diamond rather than diamond itself,
shine off sea-waves rather than the
    riotous sea-waves beneath —

angels.

Invisible light that ends up lighting up
more than physical light anyway, lighting up
whole fields of wheat as their tender shoots
   begin lengthening, golden hairs
     sprouting from earth-cheek, nurtured
      in sunlight, cooled by nighttime's
       dark, coaxed and
caressed by light-faced angels, crooned
into growth —

angels.

They look like all the ways we've ever imagined them
except sentimental, and maybe there're
   some that are sentimental as well,
      God knows —

there are fierce ones with black and green mask-faces
like the lacquered Chinese,
faces of cloudy motion with eyes of sharp light-rays,
beauty unlike any conceivable by earth-eyes,
   more glistening, twinkling, radiant,
sweeping space with expressions of light,
brought to a pitch of fineness and brightness
inconceivable —

angels.

Sifting and filtering through everything,
dimensionless, bigger than canyons of
earth and atmosphere combined, faces
wider than the seven seas, one single
   face looking down, hunting for
lost ships or wise dolphins, at the
      same time
tinier than cilia on an insect —

angels.

Capable of
slipping inside such tininess unnoticed, our
own hairs, bloodstreams, molecules, T-cells —

angels.

Faces like goblins, no, never like hob-
    goblins, faces like
natural events made even more magnificent,
cascades, strands of down-shooting
    water-glisten, shock of shook
        water-sheets, ice-light, glitter-light,
arctic brightness magnified a
millionfold —

angels.

Trickle or roar,
— and we

haven't even mentioned their
magnificent wings!

Angels.

2

The glitter of angels around waterspouts,
the flash of angels above lakes,
the darting of angels through fire-shafts,
the low flight of angels through grass blades,
the angels around children on furniture, kittens
    near busy machinery,
angels almost visible when summer heat has

    cooled and bronze sky shows a rising moon,
angels on pastures splattered with dew as a
   few cows meander toward
    a water trough,
angels on a battlefield unscrolling banners of
    cool electricity
above bloodshed, pointing to dark doors and
   doors of enlightenment in the
    midst of canon fire,
angels that touch down with gliders and parachutes
tiptoed on earth again before gravity
    sucks them down,
angels underwater moving their huge immaterial
  wings through dark purple undertow,
    swimming with whales,
angels at open windows onto streets through which
  poets look out of their hearts,
angels with widows fingering the diaries of their
   deceased beloveds,
angels with brute race car drivers as they round
  hairpin turns on two wheels and
    fervent prayer —

angels pop out of nowhere with the glistening
   membranes of their wings
    enfolding the petitioner whose own
      insignificance has just
        dawned on him
glancing at a crow on a tree branch by the
racetrack as his
race car bursts into flame.

The silence of the wreckage in the aftermath
    — the heartbeat of angels.
The "O" of their angel mouths totally engulfing the
    astonished spectators. A
  wingtip of immortality's outbreath
brushes the cheek of his 2-year old child at the
    moment of his death.
Angels sweep wings along the ruts in the track
that ended in disaster
the way a doctor sutures a wound or
  sand is smoothed by
    incoming tide.

There are angels in droves above cities besieged by
  intruders,
they take up the dead who've blossomed into
    fountains in their arms,
they transport the wounded in wings that look like
stretchers shouldered by grim-faced survivors,
they drive to the edge of a cliff in an
  armored vehicle and look like a
    half-crazed adolescent
      who's just defended a house
        singlehanded.
It's one angel divided into infinite splinters,
infinite angels doing the task of one
as if one angel did it, one

angel alone in all
circumstances
whose face is a mirror on earth that

reflects the bright
   clouds of the
      highest heavens, and whose
hands are more soothing than the
rivers of Paradise to the
hot cheek on earth that has

felt their angelic gesture!

3

They call us
   through waves of grass
      or fold of sea waves,
through mouths as tiny as mites —

they call us, thunderous
      roar that straightens our
shoulders and dusts our
   hair with white electricity.

If they were to lay flat along walls
   we'd feel our way by them, but they're
in their realm quite easy,
energized by their specific commands, while we are

footloose and stand with our
      fingers on our chins in indecision or
down on all fours with our heads on the ground
pleading for our lives

before the Tremendous Doorway
whose hinges are invisible except
    to the mind of the heart.

Angels trickle at each side of us like streams.
Angels run at each side of us like a
silken wind out of the east.

They are visible only by the time-frame of
   another time, angelic time,
so that anything of them that can be seen here, in
    our time, faces, wings,
glittering feet, shimmering annunciatory hands,
has jutted out past the edge of their time-frame
into ours — so infinitely less tremendous,
  slow motion abyss of the daily round
instead of the fathomless shale and anthracite
    plummeting abyss walls illuminated by
suspended burning quartz crystals of the
   angelic realm which
hangs over a celestial Grand Canyon-like
    counterpart to the earth-realm,

and angels stream into it and out of it day and
night without sound, no swish of tail or
sweet squeek of those
   great wet eyes opening and closing!

No high-pitched a cappella tone of their
great wings sliding
   together and apart!

                                                          8/4-9

OCEAN CITY, NEW JERSEY

The proposition that man should walk on
   two legs was accompanied by
      shock and awe among the rest of the
animal kingdom, who bowed their pretty heads in
assent and twitched their tails only
once in envy, and by

bands of angels swooping down to catch a
glimpse of this wonder. Like a
   continuous waterfall, angel faces
descended before the face of man
and continue to do so to this day
this many millenniums later
as men, women and children walk back and
forth on the boardwalk fronting the
Atlantic Ocean in
Ocean City, New Jersey.

The air, the bracing air, is filled
with invisible presences.
They have nothing to do with my mood
or your complaints. Everywhere we go, in fact,
   invisible presences are at work.
Throughout these squat and wooden stairway-fronted
   gray and white clapboard houses with
green awnings on the Jersey shore,
ancient invisible presences are guiding the
hands and minds of their inhabitants, fleeting or

   permanent, having just
arrived for the weekend
or actually living here day after day, leathery
sun-broiled skin and smelling of
coconut lotion.

Having been given bipedalism and a heart and
    head of invincible genius
what each of us does with it until we
lie down in our sand-trough of earth to be
washed by the sea of the Next World
is crucial each moment, and can
turn the tide of our lives as well as
the tide of life on earth.

A firefly of true thought in a dome of darkness
can ignite enough illumination
to span the four quarters of the universe
and light up the night of our life here.

The birth of a singing rainbow in the heart, the size of a
fingernail crescent at first, expanding to the
arc of the new moon, then
   flung like an upside-down hammock of light
from pole to pole in which stars are
cradled twinkling their million-year-old faces,
    can take place in an instant in this
child grown to full size whose inner eye is
      continuous wonder
washed by vistas and visions both arcane and as
simple as these rigorously parallel

streets that go down to the sea

where I look now at the endless passing and
repassing of people in pastel shirts on
    bicycles in front of the
bright gray glare of the sea whose

horizon has dissolved into the
equally bright gray

glare of the morning sky.

8/16

ELABORATIONS/SIMPLIFICATIONS

Elaborations and simplifications sit on
   either side of a mirror in little
pottery jars like salves.

Angels' wings, like a billion laid-over layers of
   dragonfly mother-of-pearl iridescent oil and
      water levels like celestial shingles on a roof but
making great gear movements as of gears in a
   giant windmill
      extend across the sky and shake in the air
like an aurora borealis —
Angels' wings, like breath on a cheek,
   folding out across the sky.

His life, already a compounded unavoidable
multiple car crash with a few
large diesel trucks also jackknifed across the
   superhighway and chickens
      flying everywhere and a
   cloud of toxic gas covering the scene —

his life was a sorry mess.

The doorway swung open on its hinges of gold lion-jaws
revealing the next moments of his existence as a
cloistered garden of intertwined
   creepers and blazes of glorious
      buds through which

    the path was clearly demarcated leading to the
        flashing fountain —

the door opened, he went in, the earth stood still.

The thing itself, already a gleam of light on a
    polished object,
already a galloping back glimpsed above the
   height of pampas grass,
already a tale told by an outback cowboy in an
aborigine bar as the sun boils to its descent,
  absolutely everything that exists,
     elaborate or simple as it may be,

only a slim shadow cast on earth from a
Great Light, graspable, barely
   graspable,

a song sung by a
blind harpist accompanied by a
single harp string.

                                                  8/17

THE JOURNEY

1

No one unwilling to risk the very
   pulse in his wrist should
undertake the journey, or even any
   part of it, since the
whole is contained in
   every part of it, and be willing at
any point, after skirting the edge, to
   go ahead, no map clearly
marked, armed with only
a wedge-shaped word — the
     word Love.

For this journey is one of attraction, and
the magnetic heart of it is
surrounded by darkness. There at the

pointed tip of it, the tip that pierces
our own hearts to the backbone,
   is light.

But you feel blind until that
death tastes you. Bitter cup drained,
sweet cup upturned. Turned back over. Filled.

For others to drink from.

2

Many long nights. Many days of blasted heat and
cold. No one is prepared for it. All the
careful previous descriptions are by people
before the actual journey begins, even if they
    appear, to themselves, to be
writing a memoir, or an instruction manual
based on their experience. The journey

hasn't really begun. It's only a
    dazzling Lyre Bird out of the
tropics darted by their
    bedroom window. The actual

journey is much more sober, subtle, much more
    harrowing, transformative. Leaves only
ash. Before
    returning to flesh again.

The word Love etched on all actions henceforward,
the act of love elegantly positioned throughout
    all our usual gestures, and a
heart clear of images, and
eyes filled with
simple wonders, and a
tongue like this one,

giraffe's tongue, elevated
but silent.

        8/23

TOP OF THE WORLD, BOTTOM OF THE WORLD

At the top of the world is a little green hat,
at the bottom of the world is an ice-cube.

Splendid buildings of pink and purple plaited grass
   populate the temperate middle band.

Lookout towers with leading-edge electronic equipment
   form a seeing belt of equatorial vigilance.

Under foreheads of turf in perpetual scowl
  small rodents quiver and lick tiny paws,
round beady eyes eager for new faces,
   solicitous and gentle with old.

On a canopy of rainforest boughs and preposterous branches
birds of the most extravagantly iridescent plumage
disport and display themselves to excited mates.

Long silent puddles reflect back blinding silver clouds and
  a deep black sky.

Towering trees bursting with bright edible fruit
  bend and sway above burrowing armadillos.

Heavy machinery sits idle among redwoods with rusted
  keys still in their ignitions.

A woodpecker sends its Morse Code rat-a-tat

    ubiquitously for miles.
Raw edges of tectonic plates undersea scrape each other's
delicate surfaces suggestively. Deep fissures in the sea
    deeper than did ever plummet light
go so deep only wriggling, utterly serene
    finned creatures
  take leisurely fluttering swims
    through them
      to unknown destinations.

Cadillac hood ornaments gleam in smoggy afternoon glare.

Herds of llamas on cliff-sides shimmer white
    dew-sprinkled wool in gray morning mist.

There's no one here to celebrate your
breakthrough into compassionate understanding
of how the littlest atom works its way across
wonderment to achieve apotheosis except the

traveling atom itself in the
shiver of its own excitement,

and that is God's glance of love enough
to cover you in all the

glory you'll ever need
for an entire lifetime.

8/25

BOREALIS SKY

The shush of the ocean
  roars under my bed
as I sit writing in my underpants
with the syncopated chirr of crickets out the
    nighttime backyard screen door darkness,

a fifty-four year old man still bent on the
same old thing he was bent on at twenty-one, to open a

breach and go through it, wide enough for
anyone who wishes to come, it being
not my own but everyone's, the heart's
gates into a world of
    Light, a
molten sun sitting over my bed, dripping its
     blood onto my pillow I
cover with my sleeping mouth —

the ice-cap's on the roof, the rug is a
   rustling prairie,
large animals loom, their shadows
  thrown across the room
toward me are of no
concern as I write faster than the
tsetse fly can germinate, the
  malarial mosquito bite,

dipping my pen point into wells of inky cloud,

writing the whale's testament,
hoping every day for an end to this
illusory materialistic nonsense so we can

accompany each other into the
world pure hearts envision, pure
thought engenders,

sweet ideas like giant globes
    slowly and buoyantly

rising through a borealis sky.

8/28

SLEEP AND WAKING

Sleep takes us into past time,
waking takes us into future time.

When our heads hit pillows
  they sink down through Pleistocene
    tissues —
when our eyes open they open onto
Things To Come.

We swim in sleep in the conch swirl of
  chaotic timelessness, in a
pocket of psyche and mentality
somewhere behind us.

Open eyes with the sunlight of hard objects
    bright all around us,
we see past items recognized or unrecognized
to as-yet unformed and unfathomed
oncoming realities.

Here they come! Furry-faced and
grinning! (I'll
meet you for dinner in an
  hour. Wear your pearls!)

I sleep against tall surf and sharp rocks of
ancientness. Don't ask me to name
the flying creatures heading towards me according to

mythological tradition. It's enough

they have stag horns
and blazing yellow eyes

and wear their
hearts on their sleeves!

8/29

SOME SPIRITUAL SECRETS

A green moon signifies rain.
Blue grass grows on the underside of rectilinear
    rocks.

Savages have taken away the night and
replaced it with a square wheel.

A birdcage left by an open window will attract
landscape architects from intermediate zones

and this is just
    the beginning

who has seen no paraphrase
and lived through the flames with a

   blackened mouth and tongue
       of live coals.

A horse with mane of ice stands
    solitary on the tundra

and this is
    just the beginning.

The books open and
    music is heard.

A BIZARRE EPISODE CONCERNING STIGMATA

The bannisters down the spiral stairway shone with a
    galactic intensity
as the satin-covered German matron who'd
manifested the stigmata one October afternoon
and was bleeding profusely from her palms, side and
    feet from tiny round wounds

was carried down it on a litter punctuated at all its
corners by aquariums of live baby alligators
sloshing in their greenish water slightly in the sunlight
        through the tower
            windows, down and
    down the slowly rounding
        spiral to the awaiting
papal judges and administrators below
standing abruptly and both distractedly and
    expectantly on deep red carpeting
each with rosary clicking furiously in hand

and as she bumped down stair by stair carried by
one man with hair lip and one with limp and
    glass eye
she looked up at them lined there like
members of a formal military organization
awaiting the chance to test and pass judgment
    on the authenticity of her
mystical experiences, and surveying them slowly from
left to right as her litter was set on the floor

before them,

she tossed back her head with its tousle of unkempt
    black curls

and laughed!

9/10

NEW ONSET ATRIAL FIBRILLATION

1

Here I am in a hospital bed hooked up to
saline drip and a heartbeat monitor
   seismograph zigzag green light line that
travels forward as long as I do, with its
jumpy leaps and valleys,
clear plastic tube needled into my right hand, taped
     above the wrist,
medicine to bring the tango-like boom-booms of my
   heart, the atrium bag-of-worms
electrical all-over-the-place shooting of energy that makes
the heartbeat irregular, back into regular pattern.

One minute lying on my bed at home touching
   fingertip to chest to feel the fluttery thumping,
next minute surrounded by strangers in green smocks
behind a reasonable smokescreen of professional
     respectability
seemingly knowing what they're
doing, going about it with a kind of
   jaded authority, taking my pulse,
     taking a few tubes of my blood,
taking it all in stride until I get
faint and perspirey and my
   blood pressure drops — then the
     bells and whistles go off and they respond with
accelerated alacrity of efficient

    care, each doing their
cutting-edge best to intervene in circumstances
beyond all our control, but they
bring to bear their expertise on my
    unpredictable body, and I
am turned and prodded as if
    already a corpse in the
        hands of its washers, readying it
           for the grave —

for as we are born from the womb and go
into our graves at death we are
creatures of encapsulation in these vulnerable
    physical casings,
and in a moment of panic or nausea
may forget our Sublime Creator and Supreme Help Who
first set us jumping and even now lovingly electrifies our
    very heartbeats into

melodious existence!

2

Everywhere on the planet
people are falling, falling over onto the street,
    falling out of
  tall buildings, falling over bridge-railings into a
    rushing stream, falling out of
planes with defective parachutes —

everywhere on the planet people are
falling, sliding, pitching over into plate glass windows,
falling down stairs, falling forward onto tables,
    falling out of chairs —

everywhere people are being
killed and fall where they stood, or as they were
    walking, falling off mountaintops
       into thickly wooded ravines,
people are faltering and falling, some are
    getting up, some stay where they lie —

people all over the entire globe are
falling out of their boats at dawn or in the
    dark, falling off roofs,

and I'm lying in an intensive care unit of the
    cardiac division of Osteopathic Hospital
in a strange mechanical bed, tended by
serious specialists with big personalities, and

I haven't fallen, and
God's breath is bathing all across me
as it breathes across all falling bodies everywhere

in all our diagonal trajectories

slowly or more quickly to our

appointed horizontal destinations.

3

As we grow old we become
   more like wood or stone
flinty and dry and
   windblown — wrinkled and gray-haired,
lax, slower, like those
present-day creatures from prehistory that sun themselves
   on Galapagos rocks —
taking the air —

internal organs on a downward spiral, after a
   lifetime of loyal service, beginning to
wince a little at their accustomed work —

there they are inside us in their
   orderly jumble, plugged in and
humming as they do
24 hours every
day of our life, like a menagerie of imported
   exotic beasts who
somehow all get along through
all kinds of weather — sometimes, it's true,
roaring hungrily at feeding time, or
   baying inexplicably at
     the moon —

they are our silent witnesses, advocates for our
endless physical continuance at the
great trial in God's cloud-banked courtroom —

but then they begin to
   tire, or start
      losing their grasp of the facts
(pulsate, relax, discharge electricity, go lax)
and the body, bewildered,
   staggers a little, or
      lies down.

The spirit fills with light —
no exhaustible organs there,

no secondary Source for the soul!
Light flows into it

   direct!

4

What is the heart, the muscular
   clencher and releaser, the
      four-chambered nautilus inside us,
our most intimate flesh-friend, who
   accompanies us into our darkest and
      brightest places? Our
perennial rhythm-section presided over by
usually blissed-out angelic musicians keeping a
steady beat with the brushes, a few
   stick-rolls and occasional
      high-hat, but normally
nothing fancy. But that fancy enough for all the

complex rhythms we get ourselves
   into in our daily
      diminuendos and crescendos,
   always that steady beat...

Four chambers, conveniently located, like a
   dovecote for phoenixes,
left and right atrium chambers above,
left and right ventricles below,
blood coming in in a gentle
   whoosh through the vena cava, gets a push
from the right atrium to the right ventricle, up
   through pulmonary arteries to the lungs, and
now bright with oxygen
down into the left ventricle,
up into the left atrium and
   out into the oxygen-needy body, thus
   maintaining circulation, a kind of
futurist city-plan, a cosmic four-chambered
   map of how things work, a definite
perpetual motion machine at the heart of things until the
motion goes still,
streets become empty, tall
   towers go dark, sky fills with
     a blinding light that goes
       on forever.

But the heart is also
a long line of white geese across flatlands in Denmark,
a discovery of liquid amber in a dead tree,
a sudden unexplained light like a

billion diamonds suspended in the
chambers of a million interconnected subterranean
    caverns at once!

The whole blessed history of mankind from the
first time someone stopped to actually
    look at a sunrise
to those dusty human footprints on the moon,

the attraction and propulsion of divine
    breath, the sometimes
tiny, sometimes overwhelming
intellect-bursting pure inspiration that showers
up and down through us at particular moments,
    flashing us
        entirely away —

resonating drum of wisdom
calling all shamans and saints to the
    giant iced-over lake like
  spilled quicksilver under a full moon,

the place this poem comes from, awesomely and
    mysteriously,

the place it dives into
sweet honey in another
    receptor!

                        9/11-13
                    (Osteopathic Hospital)

BOOKSTORE COFFEE SHOP

1

While we were in the bookstore coffee shop this afternoon,
me having a decaf after intensive care hospital stay of only
three days ago, I looked to my left, an
   enviable table by the tall window,
and saw an obese man with curly black
  hair and beard and thick glasses
writing very swiftly and confidently in a large
    blank-page notebook
and just like me he also had a copy of
 "The Best American Poetry 1994" on the
table in front of him, and I would have been
doing the same if I hadn't had my wife, young
daughter and her girlfriend with me,

had had in the back of my mind as we were
driving to the bookstore this sunny Sunday
   that I would get a
poetry book, buy some decaf, read a few
  poems to swing open the Gates of Perception a little,
then write a poem that was brighter, wider, sweeter and
wiser than any in the book, and now in

clear blue shirt of celestial imagination
in a parallel universe to mine, but surrounded by
  solitude, open space all
    around him for the muses and angels of

pure delight to
  play their heart-shaped harps and
    bang their slow tambourines as if
      through water
was this imagined poet writing what I imagined
  might be a truly great poem, his
hands flying like quicksilver across the page,
(I spied the writing, left-handed with ball-point,
  slanting upward)

with such lines perhaps as:
"The delectable desserts
  showered themselves without letup
    on the gratefully awaiting mendicants,"

or:
"Across wide Savannas gazelle in sinuous herds
    execute the penmanship of flight,"

or:
"Mountains rose up behind mountains,
  the breath of birds mingled with the
    breath of men in the
      middle air" —

lines linked in epic sweep, turning
  in on themselves in labyrinthine
    post-modernist splendor, yet as
passionate as he was passionate, seated heavily in his
  chair as if sky's weight were pressing
    down on him, but the

pressure releasing geysers of
   spray in words and images

shimmering with the
   perfect arc of their song!

2

As I left and passed by his table
I leaned down to him and said I was
going home to write a poem about a
poet writing a poem in the bookstore coffee shop
and then I would write some of what the
   poem was he was
     writing so inspiredly, making it up myself,
and before he
reacted I saw his notebook page, and the
handwriting I thought was a
hurried scrawl from two tables away had some
very elegant "y" back loops and looked
   extremely well-wrought, and the

whole poem interesting, and he
   smiled and said something about
"You should write a poem as if it were being written in a
   coffee shop about a poet writing a
     poem about a poet writing a..." and I
       knew where he was
     going with this, and said, *"Yeah, the*
       postmodern labyrinth,"

and he looked at me with round eyes and
   bushy black eyebrows through thickish
round glasses, and I
went away with an impression of how
   really great his poem might be, as well as
     how awful, but in my

envious heart it was great, and I sort of
   sensed it in a space of its own, only
     in my mind, about
   intimate relationships set against a
     landscape of poplars and oaks,
and the sensibility in the poem was both
deftly magic and dastardly tragic, dark greens and
heavy boughs hanging down, expansive and
   oppressive at the same time, and my
     thinking of it in this way was that

vision we have of real existence that always eludes us
   beyond the
lip of our own particular personal cliff-edge,
   seeing another person and imagining
them enjoying superlative happiness, spiritual
     fulfillment, no
   frustration, sensing in ourselves the
imagined dimensions of someone totally else, which is
     what love is — or is love rather
facing a mystery so totally
unfathomable in another person, that person's universe
with its own sun and stars, its
   own Supreme Deity, Who

    blesses and draws them
        near, or keeps them
           at a distance for a reason,
each road to that
   resplendent peak sprinkled with
      real gold and
    shed upon with
      real light —

or is love rather when we enjoy someone else's
   self-enclosed dimension past our
      own apprehension of it, but still see

God's unique Light shining through it
   in a continuous shower

even from our separation?

3 / The Poem

"Who it was I am thinking about, those two
who came together down the path toward me
with the same wind touching them both, rustling their
   hair as well as the
      leafy hair of poplars and childhood
        oaks behind them,

and the man in the hospital with atrial fibrillation
into whose life the poplar boughs and childhood
   oak trees also blew,

hooked up to saline drip and constant cardiogram,
along rivers that branch and fork,
along the wide road down from the family mansion,

all of us hooked by intravenous drip
to our own human ancestry, gone back only a
few years in conscious memory
but millenniums in molecular recording, genetic
   archive of all the laughing faces around
     campfires as well as
faces of shock watching a family slide down an
   abyss into a chasm of echoes so
     deep only silence reverberates
       in our present-day ears,

only a silence of poplars and oaks,
as mountains rise up behind mountains
and the breath of birds mingles with the
    breath of men in the
       middle air."

                                                   9/18-19

DEATH AND LANGUAGE

> *The voice…is our other genital organ,
> and one that partakes of both female and
> male: its dwelling is an orifice, and yet
> it projects.*
>
> — Paul Griffiths

1

Death certainly silences the tongue.
Orgasm is a little death. After orgasm
  some become chatty, some drift in a
    silence as in an aquarium
in no hurry to float to the top, face
  up or down.

The unleashing of words, the spray or spurt of them,
across distances, to touch, to fertilize
  thought, whose cracked shells
    lay all around its sudden
      increase, its tumescent
enlargement and articulation into
tiny arms and legs and perfect
    genitals of its own in its
self-contained world. This is an
  essay in resemblances. Do words'

echoes bounce back from the gray brick
wall of the world to convince us
somebody's there?

After generative energy expended, after the body's
nuclear explosion, sifting ash of the aftermath,
the lovely links of verb and noun, the lovely
crenelated abstract stained glass mausoleum
window of words like a solemn
silence in a gray day, the light shining through those
   lurid rainbow colors, reds and blues illuminating
beams into our dead hearts —

the stopped mouth is a dash, not a full stop, not a
period. The woman's period and the
   dot at the end of a sentence
have a cyclic sound and silence in common,
fertility a song that comes to a pause once a
   month for the moonlit
bloody refrain. Begun again after a
hot shower and some powdering,
the song regained, the singer again
  among the sung and unsung
     heroes of our
  silent and sound-pierced world.

Has this poem begun? My tongue
  trembles expectantly, turns in my
    mouth, feels the ridges of lower teeth, hopes to
      uncurl in a song of its own.
The quote exited me to attempt to sing.

Out of a silence beyond shattering.

2

Famous lasts words are fascinating, as if
at the very end when the last grains are
straining to sink through the glass pinhole
someone will sum up his life as if
throwing out wings for us to fly on above his
corpse into the remaining sunrises in our
    own lives, those
perfect pearl phrases enunciated with
  last-gasp precision, the tongue's last
    fructifying act, inseminating the
      silence with an embryo to set the
living thinking, or the final postcard posted from
somewhere nearby before the fateful journey to faraway. The

nearly illegible scrawl, legible or audible enough,
the final haiku, the final
stroke of genius before
    silence strikes its knell.
Beethoven's poignant: *"I shall hear in heaven..."*
Hegel's: *"Only one man ever understood me...*
    and he didn't understand me."
Gide's: *"I am afraid my sentences are becoming*
  grammatically incorrect."

A last dragonfly of sense given flight by the
tongue, a last leathery earthiness
before the soul becomes swift and airborne.
The last flame ignited in mid-air by

    speech, pilot light for
      intelligence to
    ignite once more into blue flame
for the last time,

last flicker of life through speech, the
    spirit's dance-floor, opening the
      tall doors and dancing out onto the
        cloud balcony as

the last golden light rises.

3

"Paint me upon a large collage"
  came to me as I
    was about to sleep, cheek against a
      black pillow.

And now, days later than that phrase,
continuing the poem, I'm struck with
    thoughts not about
first words and last words, but those
floating self-pontooned flotillas of meaning we
    produce in the middle, between
      birth and death, wrapped in
      fabulous wrappers, festooned in ribbons or
abrasive as sand-paper, the million or billion or so
words we utter in a lifetime (I wonder at
that statistic!), the ornate and Baroque

sentences, the haiku musings on a tree-branch or
missed bus, taxi-cab speeches, love-inflammations,
instruction manuals for our children,
exclamations popped out of a small box,
expostulations and replies, answers to
   $64,000 questions, trapeze artist
    agonized cries as the
        one we're supposed to catch misses
   and falls to his or her death on a
    crumpled circus floor, the whole

gamut of our speech like a tropical
aquarium with some large and
   feathery-finned exotics, all the way to a
    few fastidious scavengers carefully
cleaning up the algae.

Boats in flames pushed out across a black lake.

The guttural roar of a whore's laughter late at
   night on the Bois de Bologne.

A child's first brilliant articulations, looking up
   with a purely expectant face,

the submarine commander's terse and absolute
   words to torpedo that battleship,
then his consequent silence,

the experimental scientist inventor's words that
   set in motion an entirely new

apparatus for transcribing thoughts.

The 267 words of this poem, flowing across these pages like ragged clouds, clouds tinged with sunset, clouds in the depth of night

unseen, clouds full of rain,

then clear sky.

9/25-10/9

ALCHEMICAL JEWELS

On my table of books are alchemical jewels.
I look at their piles and see
   mechanical towers.
Shadows move across space.
Light falls in chunks
   big enough to build
     igloos and supermarkets.
Domes and towers, shadows and light.

On my table of books are alchemical jewels.
The alchemist's face is as large as a
   rotating wheel.
The jewel of the alchemist is
first knowing, then not knowing.
Things join together that were recently lead.

On my table of books are alchemical jewels.
Sprouting from piles, mechanical towers.
Shadows and light move across space.
Horse bones wait by the door!

11/9

SIX COUPLETS

1

A fire grew big as the trees on a hill
and consumed the whole forest with its flickering branches.

2

Your face fills the mirror of my heart's hall.
Your words ring pure in a silver vault.

3

A little shadow on the grass
becomes a palace full of happy phantoms.

4

I wouldn't have chosen to say these words
but a million years is not long enough to wait.

5

A hundred mummies in a row —
all those astonished faces!

6

The dim sun saps light out of trees and benches.
Chop sticks between teeth of a tiger gazing through bars.

THE CONFERENCE OF THE DEAD

1

The dead rose up and came and
  sat around the table trying to look
normal. But they were dead.

In a slow way, some started to talk about
where they'd come from, a few about
  where they were going. Their
phrases kept trailing off. Their
   heavy eyelids kept
    lowering, only
  lifting again with great
   effort, like those of long-time
heroin addicts. But it was their
  own personal and universal death these
dead were suffering, and it made them
   groggy. I

want to describe them in some
  unique and exotic way, with
lynx heads or dismembered hands, or
smiles of beaten gold on molded copper faces, but
the fact is they resembled
Frankenstein's cobbled and stitched
  creature more than the
glamorous allure of pharaohs or
   mummified Peruvian child-sacrifice

    victims, looking freshly
killed though many
  centuries old, still dressed in
little woven jackets, winsome-faced, sleeping.

These folk flaked away as they sat. When they
scratched, bits of their
  flesh flaked off and
    fluttered unnoticed to the
      floor.

They began engaging in earnest conversation
(from which I felt terribly excluded)
about the physical landscape of the
  place they'd all so
    recently left, its
gray, military-like dunes, its
chain-mail roads up peaked triangular mounts
and the flash of pewter lakes
and the stench.

But they had fresh fish that
jumped from glittering waters
  into their laps. Translucent and

transparent trout and
bass, ready to eat, shimmering like a northern

rainbow. Heavenly.

2

The dead go
to a place to us unknown.

When we pour water down a drain
we can see it in our minds
   spiral through tubing deep to the
     sea, see the
roots of tall trees push down.
But we can't know where the
dead go when they're gone.

They're suddenly not here, the details
   fuzzy rather than clear, the
photo-sharp place we are in with its
light and shade, street lights, shady
   deeps and bright
     edges
gone along with them, left to us, walking around
in our loss. One perceiver less!

But where do the dead go when they go?
This place so hard and dear, roads through
tree-lined lanes, driving to work along
back roads, sunlight everywhere.
The dead no longer here.
But where? Oh

radiance everywhere! They move in subtle

bodies of light in light very much like
they are. Or turn in a deep trough of coal through
   slothful ore. Sludge of earth —

but this is a blur.

They're where? They don't
speak to us from there. Even though
mediums, they come as
articulate air. Which is
nowhere. Ah,

people so close to us and dear, so dear,
naked or clothed, with
intricate memories and ways of
   swimming through their real
physical moments here.

When they're gone it's as if there was a sudden
shift in the air. A sudden slant that made them

disappear.

3

In the same way,
where do the living go? Down a
   street, into a
     thick wood where
shadows are taken for real, sounds are

   muffled and night descends
too quickly over the brightly seen? We in our
usual graces, stumbling in unusual ways
into each other, away from each other,
skillful at driving nails, answering letters, singing
   on key, shouting at waiters?

The small black door always visible past the
shoulder of someone we're talking to,
the mustard yellow sky always visible in the
depths of the eyes of our beloveds, as well as the

clear turquoise sky of heaven with its comprehensible
constellations, the moan of effort
as well as the sprung spontaneous
song of rapture that is the
   flip side of every darkness.

We go along these shifting landscapes, renting
makeshift rooms in their various
shady stopping places. Never for long.

Never for long enough.

Sometimes overstaying our welcome.

Sitting finally on a welcome mountaintop
to calibrate the
   sunset.

4

Life is a little map with a
   hole in it: That's us.

Sometimes we're the map, sometimes
the hole. When we're
spread out across the landscape like a
mist of light, like an
   atmosphere of clear divination,
an Unidentified Flying Object over a
   Kansas corn field spotted by a
old woman in apron and her
   blind husband,
then we're the map, easily read and followed, to a
clearly marked destination with
   interesting side roads.

When we're the hole, we're down there like
Egyptian Joseph thrown down by his
   wolfish brothers.
We're Mr. Magoo in flowery shorts on a vacation he
   can't even see.
We're the rain forests snuffed out all across the
   globe, killing off curative plants and
exotic dragonflies. We're the
Black Hole in space and the
Black Hole of Calcutta. We can go
on and on and never touch either
   bottom or sides.

God's given us the freedom to float ad infinitum
to our own destruction. Or else we're

a hole like a rent in the normal fabric, we're
a shaft of light climbing a ladder of
   animate air,
we're an emptiness that allows the
real glance of the universe to bubble up through us
unimpeded, that compassionate
falling motherly glance that
transforms us from grumpy to loving, the way

base metals could and could not

ever become gold.

                                                  11/17-19

I'M AWAKENED BY SOMETHING

I'm awakened by something in the
   middle of the night — *it's Frankenstein!*

I'm awakened by something in the
   middle of the night — it's
finally that procession of scrub-faced
   angels I've been waiting for, come to
announce to me something useful to do (probably
   be print coordinator for an
   professional education accounting company
      just like I am now — *summum bonum*, or
   a Latin phrase that means:
   *you're right where you belong right now,
      ya jerk!*)

I wake up in the middle of the night and it's the
watery ghost of my dead father, he's
come from the Land of Shades to impart
secrets to me after all, communicating through
   blue lips as he couldn't through healthy
      pink ones at all while alive —

I wake up in the
middle of the night and it's
flocks of tropical parrots to lead me around the
usual humdrum bend to a
   lagoon only glimpsed in dreams and
      vacation posters, lovers in thatched

    cottages awaiting with
  paradisiacal unguents to rub on a
    burnt out body, hush of
      superlative light cascading over
       psychological cliffs and
    dizzying heights —

I'm awakened in the
  middle of the night and it's a
golden bear on two legs with gypsy
    trainer come out of a
    starry black curtain at the
     far edge of the circus of
supernatural events to take me into
   a band of travelers who visit
    the saints along the straight
   road that leads in at
Heaven's Gate to God's
   most elegant precincts!

I'm awakened in the middle of the night by a
trigger in my own
  sleeping physiology —

   gotta pee!

11/25

THE IMAGER

1

At the edge of a great pewter sky
   sits the Imager
and way below stretch fields of bright red poppies
   blending into yellow yarrow and
luminescent mustard flowers that ignite the
     rotating light of the sun.
Lanes and country roads come to life under that
benevolent gaze. The Imager's

brows knit like cumulus clouds passing each other's
   frontiers, slipping inside each other's
     fuzz-edged boundaries, the great mist

coming down over the clarity of the scene
and giving the picture an atmospheric
steeliness. *"I have brought the small horses*
   and the hedges, the geometric
straights and curves of physical reality, and the

charmed and crystalline shape-makers of the
metaphysical map of the starry heavens and watery earth

that curves around like a kangaroo's tail
to sweep the insincere off their feet!"

There are the ones coming in in the shapes of horses,

the ones like Hokusai peasants tumbling down
haystacks, revealing their comically
   chubby buttocks and thighs, or there are
even more wretchedly, seven canisters of a

dark red powder so explosive that if, after the
detonation, everyone in the area doesn't experience
a rhinestone and pearl-studded death at the
top of a glass stairway with violin music
   wafting from down below,
then, as the manic novelist said, smiling for the
last time under the marshes, *"Nothing at all
   has any meaning,"* but chose to ignore, in
      his ignorance,
the red-tailed flock of green-necked, yellow wing'd
   parrots just landing on the moss-clinging
      cliff at your elbow
bringing the world's radiance into full view,
   popping the child's joy of existence
into the lake of immediate reflection.

These are half-asleep stanzas where I'm trying to
locate the wild man who frequents these cliffs,
get the look in his eyes when he handles the
   flowers we give him, noting his
     perception of what's before him
as if he had just put the coin into the
   binoculars at the observation lookout
      provided by the State,

to watch the tornado of voices gather force

before the bull's red eyes turn and blink.

2

The Imager leaves a host of images in full
   motion behind him as a token
     of his rapid disappearance, only to
reappear when least expected at the
next turn in the road

leaving a Gypsy landscape with gaudy vending booths of
   fruit tree orchards and yielding crops,
leaving the Industrial Revolution's cast iron
     pipes as big as
4-story houses on their sides for us to walk through,
leaving every meticulously combed hair and
     twitch of amorously nervous
   material reality for us to stroke and soothe,

that coyote Imager, laughing his yakkety laughter
as he goes, those multiple shadows his
silhouette throws into cliff walls just about to be
     totally engulfed in a fertile pink mist
and taken back into the
unseen world that waits like a fish wife for us to
return from our muddy labors
    and stay home,

the world of Light
that is God's luminous footprint,

as all images are streamed
into imagelessness again, singing a
note so vast no
sound isn't included

in its tone.

3

God is the Master Imager,
Who casts a peacock cardiogram of images past our

train windows as we pass, each of them
void, each of them as empty as the

nucleus of a molecule, life microscoped
infinitely down and down into an arena as

vast as the whole universe and its
sidereal sidecar of starry wheels,

each image also symbolic, indescribable and
inscrutable divine motions behind

corrugated glass, waltz time against a
planetary screen,

shadows chasing stags with
starry arrows tipped in

bear's blood.

The generous images flow.

The Generous and Compassionate Image Maker

Who casts each image

in fool's gold.

12/1-3

THE SENTENCE

1

The sage sat in his little tent, swatting flies.
Each fly had on a false nose.
Each fly knew the catechism of flies, and
   one among them had been to Italy.
They buzzed around his head, teeming with
    ideas. He mistook them for
 ideas. They made loops and
circles and sudden straight lines, and at
one point actually wrote out a
   sentence in their
     seemingly erratic flight.

He read the sentence, his thick eyebrows
rising and falling, his lips
silently articulating the
   astounding words made clear to him
out of the insect realm of
usual ambiguity.

2

He closed his book.

He'd had enough of history and human duplicity.

All his life he'd pondered the verities,
all his life he'd pursued avenues of
love and righteousness.

In one sentence scribbled in the
   afternoon air of his tent, light
filtering in at an
     angle illuminating it for a
       split second

everything he'd thought about and so
ponderously concluded
  evaporated as quickly as the
sentence itself, flashed and then gone,

and a new possibility presented itself to his
mind, bathing him from head to toe in a kind of
birth-cheese of neural tingling, a snowfall of
articulated thought, a presence like
the feel of mineral spring water in a
    summer pool, as if a
      lichen had grown on him with
        strange curative properties for

people suffering amnesia.

3

The sage sat in his little tent and to the
   outsider seemed no different.

He sat with his palms on the ground,
    cross-legged, face composed.

The world around his tent continued
   chewing and swallowing.

The world continued going into and coming out of
Technicolor clarity and nighttime homogeneity,
seasonal changes and momentary apotheoses of
   weather and atmosphere into a
     day so serene and golden, followed by one
       brutally cold and
         changeable.

There was one fly in particular that
   landed on his tent pole.
This fly would have yielded strange secrets to the sage
  if it had been possible, on a
   one to one basis, to
question it in some way, scientifically,
    psychically, to enter into an
interior dialog with it past all
obstacles of species and the
   disproportional time factor inherent in
a fly-for-only-a-few-days interrogated
however sympathetically by a
human-of-X-number-of-years!

This fly wasn't the consciousness behind the
composition of that sentence, but it was
one of the mechanisms of that consciousness, and it had

somehow been miraculously aligned to that
consciousness so that it was a

matter of the subtlest semantics to
distinguish that fly's individual consciousness
from the Consciousness that
  initially directs and
    consequently makes

perfect sense of

everything.

                                             12/17

BLUE SCARF OF LIGHTS

I'm sitting in this river
when I should be drowning in the
 middle of the sea,

I'm humming this song
when I should be bellowing my lungs out
 reaching the highest rafters of sound,

I'm sitting in space listening to the rumble all
 around me
when I should be freefalling among the
 kaleidoscope of the greater stars.

My heart's beating in its conservative rhythm
when it should be flung as high as an
Inuit on sealskin blanket held by the
 tribe until he passes by the
 white disc of the moon, and
  still ascending —

We're in our own claustrophobia
as morose as laboratory mice
while the calliope gears of heaven plunge and rise
 right next to us in an
  adjoining universe, and we in this one
go by clues that something's strange
when an ant carries
a thousand times its weight!

There's a blue scarf of lights that
   drifts into the room
and twists in space to become
   the sidereal world of far stars and
fiery galaxies.

I become the ruby of intense enjoyment
with my face feeling their twinkling breath, the
exhalations of angels, among
the tall clouds of adversity.

There's the universe!

Here's the steps I've taken: *little*
   duck waddles!

Where is God's Light
to illuminate

the unreachable corners?

                                                    12/23

GOD'S OBSERVATION WINDOW

It's 4 a.m., and you'd think that
   waking up out of sound sleep at this hour
you'd find God's own observation window sort of
   hanging in the air to look out of at the
wondrous workings of the world,

a time-space x-ray window seeing through the very
   curvature of the earth to the happy
   animals of Eden, the riotous
waters of the Flood, the glorious
   rise of Babylon and
the treacherous fall of Troy, the faces of early
   people full of early anguish, later
faces of struggle and French liberation, out of the
   air, down in the
     deeps, of ocean or volcanic rock,

a window at this early hour
filled with the copper rainbow glow of Australian
   sunsets, desert
heat with its pitiless blank, its
   oven-like vapor,
people on the move, nomads even
   today, the
unbelievably strong-hearted women, men with their
head cloths wound across their
   mouths,

God's own viewing porthole, suspended
   somewhere in the room by chance
when I wake up this early in the dark,
with waving pointillist wild flowers on a hill, spectral in
    color, foil shimmerings of
      light and pinpoints of brightness,
   angles of purple shadow from deep-sea rock where
sunlight is feeble, space-movement of
    star debris, regurgitations in
total blackness of dust spray from original
   creation, the sparks still
flying even this
late in the game, this late in

flickering cosmos, flickering a few more
tumultuous millenniums before flickering out,

at God's observation window
five minutes after 4

    in the dark.

12/24

FOLK POEMS

1

It was an old day
and a new night.
Life rolled on its side
and put its paws up.
The bride sat down in the snow.

Weather blew hot and cold.
That was what weather was.
Her blood dripped slowly.
So much lost that had gone before.
In one rash act.
She died. And did not die.

The snow stretched for miles.
All that whiteness
(I almost said "witness")
and nowhere to hide.

Her face of a doll's
so still now.
Blue as the ice.
Private face.

Hoot owls roosted.
Cows chewed.
Seasons came and went.

Her bones shone.
Where was he now?

Teaching school in Michigan?
Pulling trees on a farm?
Lost in the hills?
He won't show his face.

Where is the moon now?
Still in the sky.
The earth still revolves.
Everything's changed.

Birds still alight
on sycamore branches.
He can't remember.
She can't think.

The snow has melted.
The ground is soft.
The sky has a dark tinge.
Her laughter subsided.

The breeze picked up little things
and moved them around.
The bride of the night
wore a black veil.

2

The rainbow arched
in the cup of his hand.
He threw it in the air.
That's how it got
   stuck there.

They saw it as they headed home.
They saw it over the pine forest.
They gauged the distance remaining
when they saw it over the lake.

"I can't understand people,"
said Mr. Raccoon to his spouse.
Mrs. Raccoon kept on chewing.
"I wonder if they understand us,"
he said, as the rainbow
sprang up over some trees.

The wolf man stood up by the campfire
and the family of twelve travelers froze.
One saw God come and take him.
Little sister thought he was funny.
Father tried to negotiate.
Wolf man's teeth flashed in the firelight.

What happened next only the owls know.
Wolf man's eyes shone in the firelight.
One saw God's eyes in those sapphires.

They all felt the gaze of great forces.
Wolf man turned into a pack.
Each wolf of the pack was ravenous.

The rainbow arched over the moon.
It looked like a raised eyebrow.

Dust mixed with cinders and sparks.
Blood mixed with dirt and saliva.

Each one felt God's grip directly.
Each one let out a shout.

Each shout hung in air like a rainbow.
The night was an arcade of rainbows.
Each spirit was wearing a rainbow
as it floated above the campfire.

3

The hairy mammoth stomped the turf
We sang to him through the long night
The white owl flew over black lagoons
My love sat still and would not move

Click-clack the brambles broke in the pit
The mammoth bellowed and stomped
The moon the death-white moon
poured milk on the hills
poured light on the flatlands

My love sat still in the bellowing moonlight
Her trance had fumes and licks of flame
She saw our houses go up in flames
She saw God's Hand come down and quench them

I put her in front of me on the horse
We rode on ground as hard as light
His hooves made a clatter that repeated twice over
We rode for two days until she woke up

She woke up at dawn as the moon sank down
I turned the horse and we walked our way home
The mammoth was silent down in the pit
We slept for two days and then woke up

We joined the feast and sang the songs
She told what she saw as the white owl flew
The people listened and agreed to move
Their folded hands their solemn faces

The moon poured milk on the hills
poured light on the flatlands

1/13-17

THE EXCAVATION

They came and carved out his insides, excavated him
   like a papaya, like the
     hard football seed of an avocado,
they excavated him entirely, left him limp on a chair
which was fine with him, he was
    ready to be emptied.

They took out the Zebra Preserve where
   black and white stripes of beast lined up
     with black and white
       stripes of material world so that
         both disappeared.

They divested him of the
   stairway down into the neurological
      gloom that he sometimes
   strolled down or fell down
     or got pushed down by oppressive zephyrs —
out it came with a terrific creaking of stubborn
   nails and tooth-and-groove planks
     intrepidly cohering.

They removed the antique telephone switchboard, the
    lines as dead as shale,
his self-esteem stripped away like old
   wallpaper, faded patterns of roses,
     hackneyed designs of pirate ships & anchors,
they zipped away his recollections of green butterflies on a

      camping trip just before
        poison oak, just after
          learning to swim.

They pulled out the long spaghetti strips of
   adolescent lust still flexible and
      noodle-like, post-adolescent
angst and philosophical sexuality from the
fog-and-sweat bound pages of Dostoyevsky, coupled with the
Halleluiah Chorus of adulthood with its
school teacher choir-mistress
      who sometimes shows her leg —
they even stripped off the drier outer bark of
old-age-back-to-lust-in-the-mind
       that cracks as it bends, waggling a
   discrete Eucalyptus branch or two,
pungent and green,

and he was perfectly all right with this,
he was actually relieved, he felt unencumbered although
    a bit empty (when lust vanishes, some of
        the world's glitter goes blah)...

Then they took concepts, half-concepts, incipient ideas and
   random twitchings of brain-stem,
some of them harking back to early prehistoric times —
    what an iguana fifty feet long might think as it
      suns itself on a rock —
they peeled these away one by one, and each time they did
the world underwent a colossal transformation,
   warping with cello scrapes one minute,

wrapping around itself to piccolo notes the next,
    becoming a dancing dot in space,
   a ribbon of torqued light over an
     abyss of black flame-tongues
accompanied by the booms of mammoth elephants in heat —

all these illusory constructs they stripped away from his
  delicate insides: the shape of the universe,
    the height of the sky, the length of a
     day or a moment, thoughts on
  love and death and procreation —

they were all excavated angelically with a silvery authority
and he grimaced as his most cherished imaginings were
  taken, but each time his face registered a
    deeper kind of ultraviolet beneficence,
     his eyes looked like stars twinkling up from the
      bottoms of wells,

and he began not to mind this latter
  excavation at all, but began to
help them by leafing through old
    student notebooks and cherished diaries:
"Here, don't forget this!" "Hey! did you forget
  the one with the diagram? Did you forget my
    thesis on the shape of the universe
     as a Rose?"
until he was hollowed of concepts and
  frail intellectual constructs, and when it was
    done the world shone with its
own true innocent light, quivering slightly

like the sleek fur of a mouse at dawn
   hurrying through dewy grass blades in search of
      seeds —

he was naked from the inside out like a
flame of quicksilver standing up from a pool of light,
quivering in the mesh of pre-dawn breezes —

he saw how crucial this excavation could be,
he saw the parade of little 3D pictures that
   went the way of forgotten memories and
     5-alarm fires, air filled with
   the falling cinders of cherished mementos,
     irreplaceable snapshots and
       nostalgic plaster of Paris objects from childhood
         gaudily painted —
he saw that this was part of every revealed system of
concavity to the universe's convexity into the
     world of pure spirit —

he was not empty but thin air circulated where he'd been,
he was not silent but each tap of stillness opened a
   further dimension in the Building of Being both
     horizontally and vertically,
he was not so dead that his breath couldn't
   blow out a candle placed at his lips,
yet the reel-to-reel video extravaganza
     (down to the threads at his frayed collar)
billowed up into empty space like the
   glance of an enlightened being
at the suddenly

sweet-faced inquisitor come to
　　test his enlightenment and becoming his
　　　　disciple instead —

moon gone into stars, stars gone into
blank Mobius, Mobius strip become at once
a starry hairband for his head, all the
　　trapped light spiking out in
　　　　blinding rays around it

lighting up every face that beholds him
until each person on earth becomes
　　similarly enlightened and
falls laterally into the excavated space in
　　　each one of us while alive so that

at death it is simply a final smile
across lips at peace like a bow laid down,
and a heart... well,

a heart like the ones we've got beating in our
　　chests at this very moment,

these ones with dozing lion-faces snoozling
　　out from fiery cloud.

　　　　　　　　　　　　　　　2/2 (Ramadan 1)

CONTINUUM

"*If it's all a continuum,*" he thought to himself idly
at the top of the Ferris wheel overlooking
the Forbidden City in Peking with its actual dragon
   guards languorously slapping armored tails on
      Tiananmen Square, making showers of sparks —

"*if it's all links across time and space welded
   seamlessly together so that
      no one can see the discreet elements
         interknitting,*" he said to himself
as a tidal wave nine stories high licked away
   whole families of picnickers from their
      beach bacchanals, dashing some down
into leviathan deeps among briny dishwashers with claws,
      whooshing others across distant seas to
start life over in grass skirts on tropical isles —

"*I mean, if it's all a totality, a single unit with
   facets, a 3-dimensional puzzle with the
painted cubes locking into place to form
golden sunsets or dark blue explosions in the
   alchemical laboratories of the heart,*" he
continued, leaning down hard on the
ostrich's neck to keep from falling off into
      sword-sharp New Zealand grass and being
         diced to death like a raw celery —

"*if it's one element inter-tubed inside another like a*

telescope trained toward outermost space, ending up
in innermost spatial territories of wonder and supernatural
   vision where all color is super-saturated and all
     sound is excessively high-pitched but strangely
       relaxing," he was
almost concluding to himself over a
decaf cappuccino at his quarter-to-midnight
kitchen table with Raven the black cat
   licking her silky licorice body-hair and the
Greek chorus fridge doing its usual
   nonverbal commentary at stage left —

"then" (and this should be accompanied by
loud bassoons, cellos and Wagnerian tubas)
"then there is absolutely nothing that can
   happen to us nor nothing we can do
that not only doesn't make perfect sense in the
total picture, but isn't also like
a parade of royal footman in skin-tight
   purple jerkins delivering a continuous
     series of secret messages on
silver trays, lifting the lids with elegant flourishes,
revealing the hyper-astro-biology and metabiology
of each vein dilation, brain and heart-pulse both from
ourselves and simultaneously from Bengal tigers in the
   wild and on the prowl,
each message suddenly made limpidly clear by the
mere fact of being read, by
   midnight's sliver of thin moonlight, of how

God without movement

*creates all movement, Sees and
Listens without eyes or ears, Speaks a
language the subtlest DNA marvel only
   distantly approximates,*

*our own beings in contiguous motion, as
  perpetual as time, as curved, as
    rounding back onto themselves, as
turned inside-out in a flash as we*

*take one more sip from the frothing cup and
set it down again on the
  frozen ocean of the tabletop
in the rising suspended wave-crest of the room
  on the dry ocean floor of this planet*

*rotating happily through an endless
  multiplicity of moments
smiling to itself radiantly in
    deep space."*

2/2

THE PROCESS

When I write these poems
I become a bear licking honey off its nose,
  a confused navigator both
    at the wheel which spins around and
      lashed to the bow
    gazing out over dark waters —

the poem is a piece of topology
  spotlit terrain by terrain as my
motley expedition advances,
I its nervous expeditor.

I expect pythons, I expect eruptions, I imagine
naked natives in out-of-the-way villages.
I expect my head on a stick, my heart
  cut out raw and served up to some
    drooling alien god. I want

the silence of snow, the long trail
  up to Mirror Temple,
a greeting by the Invisible Saint of these
  experiments, a warm-blooded handshake as we
jointly contemplate the slow snowfall of divine letters
tumbling into words in the air as eternal as
ice-crystals just before

  blinking back again
    into blankness.

2/4

POEM WRITTEN OUT IN THE COFFEE BAR

I want to write a poem about everything and everyone
down to the serrated edge of the tiniest barnacle
   hidden under a hull, down to the
quickest blink of light on sloshing water, down to the
eyelash in the eye of the most anonymous trash-picker,

which may be synonymous with wanting to write a poem
about nothing and no one,
emptiness unrolling a plush ermine carpet up a
phantom stairway to the moon,
no one occupying no place on a phantom subway
   speeding like a silver bullet underground
     every major city in the world with absolutely
no one in any of the cars, no one looking out
any of the windows at
no one waiting in a long green overcoat and
  paper bags and afghan hound on no
    platform in anywhere, steam hanging in space,

this great desire and love for all of you, with all your
psychic spiders and neurological tarantulas,
a sweet embrace across a smoky or smokeless air
to adjust the golden halo like a head full of curls above
   eyebrows raised in perpetual
     expectation and surprise, each

halting or all-speed-ahead conversation between
two or more people, those enthralling

   enunciations, those devastatingly delicate
    "t's" and "s's," those sudden heart-stopping
consonants hovering like honey-laden bees in midair before
zeroing in on home, the loopy oceanic
  rises and falls of thought made explicit by
    words under harsh light or moonlight,
the whispers that awaken crickets as far away as
    Rangoon, that startle
      fireflies in the Adirondacks,

I want to listen in and add my own personal
twinkle to a recollection or a wishful thought or
flight of irrational fancy, I want to
pause with solemn brow at a moment of true
  emotional revelation, the
earth-shattering embarrassment of a teenager divulging
  shyness in love or hesitance in meeting,
the sexual echo like a distant wolf-howl of
    unutterable loneliness, the
peach-colored tinge of perfection in the light cast
  aslant at a moment of sensual satisfaction,
the breathless sigh of awe at a visible masterpiece of
rock or stream on green mountainside in autumn,
deer-print in snow, a cloven signature like two
  acorns tail to tail,
water drops down a window watched for the
  first time by a nuclear physicist under five,
the nose-twitch of terror by someone in an elevator
   in an abandoned warehouse thinking of his
     mother, her eyes full of tears,

and yet the list could go on and get nowhere,
the details of specific characteristics pile up until the
end of eternity and we
wouldn't have caught it, its dragonfly swiftness
    elude us,
and maybe writing a poem about nothing and
  no one would be 100% more successful at
capturing the particular flavor of Love and its
    gorgeous dance-partner Compassion in
      polar bear altitudes on roller rinks of
        arctic splendor,

the steam shot up from a fissure in the earth from which
no one emerges, no personage in
  icicle disguise, no creature taller than
Nigerian basketball player in wolf robe and
    moose-horns who knows the
      inner significance of every
        detail of the ancient rituals, and can
throw the sculpted walrus bones just so
over the inch-high glacial shaman's grid —

it's a song I'd like the whole earth to join in,
one man so insignificant, so filled with
cosmos, so star-struck, so empty of diagnosis, so
     aromatic of ecstasy,

I'd want a chorus of ferns with their
extended stiff green feather boas to join in,
redwoods with their Russian bassos, timpanies of
    icebergs and

    cymbals of streaks of light cast
       down across blue ice,

all to reach an unbreachable crescendo of
sense and consciousness just to
touch that distant comrade as yet unacquainted
  at the back of the train
    arranging his small luggage and
      double-checking his itinerary,
or that expectant dancer at the side of the stage
afraid of her stockings, already having
  performed each pirouette to
    perfection in her mind and taking her bow,

each widening or narrowing of eye of
   human alive at this moment,
each lip-parting and closing again, each
   thoughtful hand pulled
     back across sweat-beaded forehead,

those beads of salt and water pumped so
deftly from glands deep in delectable skin, somehow
  triggered by other than
 hot weather, the mysterious deftly touched
pressures of the heart,

all voices heard in clear delineation
in four-dimensional chorus
let loose across canyons of wind.

                                     2/17

EVERY POET IS FOOLISH

Every poet is foolish
   thinking words alone will
     help —
nothing can change the flight of cranes
   at that particular angle at that
particular moment in the crane-clock season,
   nothing can change the bubbling brutality in the
heart of man, cudgel-fist raised in
    boozy squalor at the
 dribbling base of civilization, drool from
angry lips that if only they could say and pronounce
words of neon sparklers on dazzling strings about
a herd of wild stallions galloping free through
    sunrise gorges to the sea,
or sweet words of lovers on piled-up pillows
   inside a house of storms, waterfalls
twelve miles high cascading on their roof, flames rising
right outside their windows,

but their sweet words enough
  to silence the thunderous crash
and quell the flame's heat
and transform both into
gong-music softly plonking, softly melodious
   down a long hallway of reed-breezes
     below a flight of cranes and the
nervous-sounding song of chickadees looking for seeds —

"if only the world brought to light by words,"
says the foolish poet holding his feet and
rolling down moss hillsides to moo-music,

*"if the hearts of hearers could only lend ear to
   our songs of light and despair,"*
foolish poets the world over sing as they
   slice another slice from a bread loaf of stone,

*"if only what rolls off the tongue articulated with
   care and rapturous carelessness,"* say
poets balancing on tall cliffs with their
   arms out at each side like dragonflies,

and suddenly people peering out of windows raise their
   blue hands to their faces and smile,
the man who's doffed his overcoat and stands on the
   girders of a suspension bridge
      gratefully climbs down, hugs his loved ones,
the poor child tastes honey-crackle and fresh
   strawberries in his watery porridge,

*"because the Universal Grammar has put forth some
new green branches,"* the foolish poet says,
and the poet, rolled tightly into a ball right now
indistinguishable from hedgehogs and surprise
   Chinese toy baubles (unwrap the
      paper streamers and out fall
galloping stallions running free through
   sunrise gorges to the sea,
sweet words of lovers on piled-up pillows

rubbing their sweet eyes filled with
soft light of dawn's worlds, silver light and
   blue light filtering in through
curtains of poets' words
pouring slowly down like fresh rain on a
   windshield,

the shine of loving prophecy lighting up the
toughest corners in the most
abandoned dwelling-place), *"if only these*

foolish words, each one the seed of more
   flowery worlds,
were taken as seriously as TV songs about
new cars or TV slogans for ice cream,"
says the poor poet whose face has become
almost edible as it dissolves into the background
   atmosphere, those

jeweled words echoing dimly now,
those dancing verbs and jewel-like nouns
beginning to echo with a tinny sound,

the foolish poet sitting by the roadside naked

talking to stones.

2/22

AH, THAT UNSEIZEABLE MOMENT

To seize the moment,
fling a swift switchblade into a glass pumpkin
   and it bleed juice,
just past the edge of exhaustion,
to seize the moment that comes
   circling up the spine, just as in
the writing of this poem — I was feeling
   overcome with a certain mustiness, but somehow

the clong in the chest struck mallet against gong
to seize the moment by whatever
horns or tail available, and
go into it, one step farther, push aside those
   heavy draperies and as
     excited as ever walk deep into the
       middle of the vaporous room of
the moment, see what statuette might be
surprised on what pedestal in what shaft of
afternoon sunlight with what
sinister fingerprints on it, or

what sweet apricots nestling in a crystal dish on
what sunlit windowsill, what
pauper-poor philosopher living under stairs appear
   holding an umbrella of flying doves
crossing a street of rushing waterfalls
standing in midair suspended on a
   thought of ultimate

    origins and destinations, one
  poised eyebrow raised, one
    quizzical mouth awry,

and he lean forward into the mirror of our hearts
surrounded by green leaves of a particularly
   atmospheric kind, and with a
single finger write out the
   meandering story of our lives with a
     few flicks and backstrokes
       on water, scattering a few
     mists and water drops to the edges,
getting through all the algae and overgrowth that
makes of the heart a less than transparent place of
worship and intoxication, level by
   level up goose-wing stairways unfolding

to this moment seized,
this moment spinning around itself, humming

obsessively to itself, yelling its
unknown name out loud and it echoing for at
   least ten minutes

on the sunlit tip-top crag
of Surprise Peak.

2/24

HISTORY LESSON

"What is history, then?" he asked, tapping his
   atomic pencil on the spine of the
      Book of Hours, fiddling with a
   glass thimble, and out of its circular
shadow rides a horde of cavalry with streaming banners,
their metal visors down, their horses snorting,

"but a series of setups and betrayals," he added
   pulling at a lugubrious moustache, arching
      ogival eyebrows,
and suddenly the walls were a riot of rabble demanding
heads be cut and blood be shed, although
      never their own,
and the ceiling dropped down while opening up to the
crashing of ocean waves cut in two by the
   prows of fleets of hastening ships, thirsty for gold,

"annexations," he continued, twirling his fingers on
   a disk of concentric black circles like the
      rings of Saturn,

*"forced conversions, colonial takeovers, monopolistic
   mergers under one flag,"*
his door opened up and lines of goose-stepping children
   filed past his desk averting their
      eyes in his direction then
snapping them forward again once they passed,

"and, of course, adulteries, incests, wife-beatings,
   brother or sister poisonings, mother or
      father murderings, hanky-panky with
         foreign royalty, sending
   emissaries off to certain death,
doom, despair and the
   degradation of the human spirit," he
sighed as he climbed onto Geryon's back and
flew off to a deeper rung of Hell, Virgil teetering
    before him,

"and yet," the light dawning on him, aslant from on high,
"there is one way that history becomes a
single shaft of vertical brightness
landing at our feet, inviting us to
   step into its tubular being
in time and
   out of time,"
he said, opening his shirt-front and the
   dazzling cylinder appearing like a
      Gypsy dancer, flamboyant, alive,
turning its light against historical darkness,
churning all the atomic energy of
     historic event into
     non-historical verticality,

a little dust cloud
   whirling around it with low
Tibetan humming, deep Arabic intonations, high
   Gregorian plainsong, chorales of
     itinerant angels with piccolos,

he winked one wink out of the whirlwind
and took off, coattails disappearing
    inside that cylinder,
guillotined heads rolling down along the cobblestones,
charging horses flecking foam into the wind,
war crashing overhead,

he smiling obliviously, his heart a
    dome of sufficient
        beneficence,

his historical
existence done.

                                                            2/26

ARE WE HUGGED BY ANGELS?

A ship winks out over the horizon:
  is it just traveling on,
    or dropping out of sight
      down an abyss?

An ant backtracks after
  bumping into a foot:
did it just bump into *"something"*
or into a monstrous foot?

Sheep in a green field
    grazing:
they've been standing still for hours,
or are those white humped rocks?

Earth turns in its orbit in space:
  is that really zillions of
    miles of nothingness,
or are we an eye in an eye socket
      gazing at itself?

We walk around on earth
  until we die:
are these close encounters with
    total strangers
or are we all one family circulating in a
    single womb?
Have we all met before in the Soul World

and just now recognize
   that the light's been switched on,
or are we really solitary and
   miserable, banging on
     death's door?

The sun shines on
   grass blades at our feet:
does the earth stand still
    beneath us?

Are we hugged by angels?

                                                 3/2

WRITTEN DURING A RAINSTORM

Just suppose the most torrential rainstorm ever,
rain through trees with high winds, rain
   dripping in individual disastrous drops
     through ceiling onto floor while
rain sloshes continuously outside the window
as if readying for the Flood all over again, but this time
   no survivors but cockroaches,

rain filling the eye sockets of the dead,
rain in sheets connecting soothsayers from
   Kuala Lumpur to Timbuktu,

rain so brilliantly white against storm sky inky black,
rain as if millenniums of liquid threat were
    coming true, rain of
iceberg melt, ocean rise, whale vengeance, dolphin ache,
rice paddy rebellion, down
   mountainsides of waterlogged pine trees with
    no sweet sunshine on glistening grass
      afterwards, but a

steady pounding of jagged lances of slanted
    rain down an
endlessly weeping sky until we are all
back in the water world again, bodies afloat or
   submerged, dead and alive,
our bones like primordial canoes

searching for land in vain.

                                             3/8

WHEN I PRAY

When I pray
the whole world becomes a pair of huge
   insect wings behind me, and I am a
standing green insect with metallic
   thorax, inhaling distant

zephyrs of intoxicating gas
   only a rare breed of
     insect can survive,

and when I pray the sky in front of me becomes
light and edged with silver
but the sky behind me becomes gun-metal gray
and filled with heavy storm,

and when I pray
there are negotiations on board ocean liners between
warring countries, and treaties are brought out and
   signed in triplicate, and people
     bow and shake hands, and an old
   mother in knitted shawl next to a
     cold stove lets out a deep
sigh and holds her
grandchild closer to her breast,

and when I pray I turn aside from
the chopping block, the gas chamber, the
cocked rifle, the seething self-destructive

hatred in a glance,
swollen knuckles, the poisoned pen,

I turn at an oblique angle to the
political explosion, the downing of airplanes, the
destruction of edible food,
and billows of scarlet velvet blow past the
   form of a human standing and facing God
I make when I pray, and

billows like the sails of ancient sailing ships
blow their incandescent white canvas glittering in the
   Atlantic sun of new worlds past my
figure of a man standing at the absolute
front edge of his existence, toes on the
   prayer carpet, facing God free of all that is
other-than-God
when I pray, and the world becomes
   silent when I pray, as silent as the

growing of wood in a thick forest, or the
   slow death of an old moose alone on a
     hill, or the wheeling of a
       young bird in a
sun-drenched sky,
silent as a tomb, but alive, silent as the
sea, but deeper, silent as the
   sky, for at the

bottom of the sky, with his forehead touching the
   bottom edge, is the

human figure on two straight legs facing
    one direction and praying with
        one heart of a
person praying, of me when I pray, turned like a
    gyroscope, up-ended, twirled in a
        great wheel, brought back again to the
upright position, facing
wind and ocean and fire burning down houses
and rain battering roofs and hulls of ships
and mountain-faces fluffy with mountain goats,

and when I pray
the slice comes clean through the terrible drama of
    matter, the operatic
        tensions of objects clash in space,
the suicidal psychology so intertwined with a
        desire for rebirth, and there is a

rebirth of wonder, a Bromeliad of bright pink
bloom out the middle of the silver green succulent
    leaf of the
tropical Bromeliad, and the
prayer is the rebirth of light like live lightning
out the corners of the angles of a two-dimensional darkness

and when I pray I become a
firefly or dragonfly, no, only a

man standing facing forward

to pray.

THESE FACES OF OURS

Everyone walks around with
   faces of lovers of God, *everyone,*
young, old, grumpy, delighted, enraged,
empurpled with
   rage, reddened with violent temper, drink,
despair, eyes like acetylene, blowtorch tongue and
   nozzle nose, forehead like
      perpetual landslide, no,

absolutely everyone,
cherubic and winsome, eyes bright as
flying saucers over sunlit skies in Chicago,
hands delicately rubbing fuzzy cheeks,

everyone walks around with faces of
   God-intoxicated
      creatures who know the true source of all
pain and pleasure,
each blood vessel a periscope gazing across the
   sea of God's bliss,
each vein a tributary from the swollen river of
   God's Glory, all these

beloved faces, going along their way, so
   preoccupied, whisking past without
eye contact, mouths quiet but invisibly
     engaged in continuous dialog,

but look! Out of the womb, those fresh
faces of new fruit, eyes clenched, puckered
cheeks and chins, how they
slowly flatten out like sheets of
   foolscap for writing on, and they
do get written on,
    by quill pens a mile long held by
    angels who scribble and scribble on our
faces day and night, awake and asleep,

eye-twinkles, mouth-wriggles, nose
   twitches, furrowing of
     brow, harrowing of
gaze, then the
sudden relaxation as of giant
mammals broken free from sea depths, suddenly
exultant in earthly sunlight,

faces of love or forlorn expectation, darkened with
drugs or despair, a great
   cloud passed over, rain pelting
     down on drawn eyelids,

my own face this morning so hopeless,
feeling the set of mouth and
deadening of eyes — but we're in

God's aquarium, we're
measured from His element, our
faces are puzzle-pieces in the
   entire world-picture of His

love. And each
    facial gesture shows it, each
        exchange of facial message
a pure love letter written in physical longhand

    to God.

Out of our faces great doves explode,
great stretches of grass and flamingos,
    great pampas of the
        mastodons, and out of our

glorious faces banners of light unfold, rippling
    through night sky, making their
        own aurora borealis for us
to see by, light shaking multi-colored curtains of light,

and out of every face on earth come
flares and water spray and volcanic eruptions
    of purest essentialness,
moods of mist and enlightenment of
dusty texts tucked away in Syrian libraries,

tiny exchanges of wisdom so
minute even gnats feel comfortable circling around
    in their light,

so vast no bald eagle ever gets tired wheeling
    endlessly in their sky.

        3/11

VARIOUS MEETINGS WITH THE SELF

"Who's that standing at the foot of my bed in a
    bluish wisp when I
        wake up at 5:30 a.m. in the dark?" I ask.
"Your self," is the answer.

"And who's that pushing his skeleton with
    squishy and twitchy organs all around it
        like a jellyroll out of bed to go
            take a pee?" I ask.
"Your self," is the answer.

"And who is that standing by an enormous shelf
    of tattered books
with a blue chicken in one hand
and a piece of the true cross in the other,
    blood droplets falling to the floor?" I ask.
"Your self," is the answer.

"And who is that like a blind mole with excessive overbite,
too timid to speak some moments, at other moments
ready to go into spontaneous song and dance with
twirling straw hat and revolving cane?" I ask.
"Your self," is the answer.

"And who is that gazing in silent rapture at the
birch tree loosening its papery white bark at the
first sign of spring, rips off a piece, feels it with
    thumb, its softness somehow nostalgic, and

slips it into his shirt pocket delighted?"
"Your self," is the answer.

"And who is that who at a flick of the heart's
   hidden switch could stretch himself
     out on the sky the way a bear
stretches himself out on a bed of needles in July?"
"Your self again," is the answer.

"And who, in the tubular dark of telescopic night,
plods out past the edges of the city's lights to
   tempt the dragon of forbidden
     knowledges out of his lair to share a
fiery cigarette of wisdom together
before death from inert old age overtakes them?"
*"The self you were born with and
   leave off, expand to eternity or drag to the
grave,"* is the answer, as the

night closes down, as the

dawn opens its incandescent petals like a

white flower.

                                                  3/14-16

IF YOU WORSHIP A GOAT'S HEAD

If you worship a goat's head on a stick
   whose eyeballs light up bright red when
     inspired,
then know it will do you no good when
the front door of your house blows off
and a golden light lays down a
   stairway for you to
     embark on — it
will do you no good at all.

Folds of velvet cloth slurp together
   disappearing down one of the concrete holes
from 1830 that make things vanish into
   another era (I heard "1830" distinctly
as if I were a lunatic Joan of Arc
   hearing voices...).

If you worship a floating bit of gauze over the
   city rooftops on a
sunset evening when the
   clouds look like crowds of
adolescent angels with
peach fuzz on cheeks and
   spangled wings
it will do you no good when
The Ugly bangs on the door of your heart
bringing its twin sister Reality and its idiot
   half-brother Justice and its

    loud stepmother Righteousness
into your heart's unhappy house with
    muddy boots a yard too
big for its feet —
swirling water obscures imperfections along about
1716 when all's quiet on the
    Western Front, but an
  Indonesian farmer sets fire to his
      hut and scares the
         cows.

If you worship anything but Divine Majesty, Divine
      Beauty, God's own
paradoxical Oneness, the light on a

desert floor when night's earth's been
      clicked on,

the ocean with its cabin lights, the liner
    with its phosphorescent depths,

the door that is a wall and the
wall that is a door so vast you fall
face-forward into stars —

unless this be the focus of your heart's
three-cornered love letter to the
true origin of your birth and the
joyous laughter of your destination
(I'm talking to myself now, and no one
    else on earth — the earth is still and

dim and uninhabited),

clouds like clocks and death-march wooden
soldiers fall on you all day and all night like rain,
pigeon-toed, step over one
threshold after another into rooms of
disapproval and rejection —

eliciting finally an *"Oh!"*
from your beloved's lips

as you fall through feathers
forgotten even to yourself.

THE NAKED FISHERMEN OF TINDERZEE

The poet comes to the end of his life at the
   top of a stair in a dark
      hallway.
Now cultures as distinct as the Trobriand Islands and
   Czechoslovakia warbled pretty regularly
through that poet's golden throat. Green
fountains in a glade surrounded by the
     purple and black flash of flying parrots
spurted silvery juice in higher and higher arcs.

The whale house is dark behind him, and
behind the whale house the county is dark, and
behind the county the state is dark, behind the
   state the continent with its
distinctive puzzle shape is dark, and behind the
     continent the globe with all its
inhabitants is darker still, the long-suffering Chinese
lighting their punks to fill the air with
     coils of scented smoke, Polynesians
watching the black night come down, Hindus with
rose-tinted fingers, dervish eyes, lips like gazelle eyelids
watching the light blue dawn come up,

and behind the dying poet, dying on his feet,
the darkness lengthens out farther and
     farther behind him, he can hear
distant windows being closed, through the
     closed door in front of him he hears

a stuck window being opened,

he touches the knob, or is it himself? His
    forbidden zones, the
        gnarled Africas of his emotions? His
own erection?
The door opens,

the poet comes to the beginning of his life at the
top of a stair in a
sun-drenched valley, he steps down with
cane of writhing snake, bamboo umbrella,
intergalactic coil which he uses to sweep away
cobwebs out of heaven, even out of the very
        thought of heaven — he lifts himself on
tip-toe to get a better look
and lariats of fire in shapes of stampeding bison
rumble past him in a hurry to
    nowhere,

a knife sticks out of a log, everything has
prism facets rotating and spiraling at the
    edges of everything, that he

might stop just once and take spiritual inventory of
what he's seen and
    recorded, and who was
there when the piano of his innocence collapsed, who
      bandaged the
    prima ballerina's foot with
        spider-gauze, who rubbed his

cheek like Pierrot against her muscular calves,

for she is dying now, and he is given life, she has
danced the pirouettes of pollen and
   it has taken root,

he will soon be standing among his
light bulb trees in the
orchard of his heart's desire —

radiance is breathing him.

He is sinking fast into
incandescent billows, no one to
spit on anymore, no one to

fall asleep in mid-sentence, new face coming out
refreshed among the naked fishermen of
   Tinderzee, below

bending jack fruit trees.

3/24

A HUNDRED PEOPLE IN A ROOM

A hundred people in a room. Bare
   platform stage front.

Various things could happen.

Someone could announce, with
supporting evidence, the
fiery end of the world: slides and
    charts.

Someone could heal us all of our childhood
traumas, of which
  there are so many, even so
    many more when we start to
think of them. Or

someone could let loose a hundred rabbits to
lick our ankles and have their
  silky ears scratched.

Someone could stand on the stage and slowly undress.

Someone could stand on the stage and put on
article after article of clothing until they become a
    mountain of knickknacks, Victorian
     lamp shades, debris and detritus
until we're all forced out the
    front door onto the street.

A man with one protruding eye like a
glazed grape could announce he's
king of the world, and back it up with
   subatomic particles in the
shape of robot legions 10 miles across.

A grandmotherly lady like Glinda the Good from Oz
could soothe us all into fuzzy cosmic
   optimism and wash us invisibly with a
      huge love-sponge lasting forever.

A hundred people in a room.

Each one could be the hub of rotating spokes, the
   Apocalypse-Bringer, the
      Healer of Souls. If the

walls of the room swung around to centralize
   any of us
would the universe step back and make
   room, would
visible crystal arches hover above us
held aloft on athletic angel shoulders
   to the accompaniment of the
      bass drums of heaven?

Would the huge moustache of a tyrant
   overpower us, or the
seductive silver eyes of a crooner, a
   superstar, a true lover
expressing the tremors and tremendous longing of his

or her soul for the extreme origin of all of us,
for the embrace of light from which there is no
    separation, and we are
ignited beyond our own imaginations
    into the true sea of life!

A hundred people in a room
could change the world.

A hundred people in a room.

Or one.

3/26

THEFT OF A COAT

1

In a half-dream state I revisit
  the ongoing saga of the theft of my coat,
taking me to Russia, hallways of brown mist,

further clues. Although there was
never a coat, and
no theft of a coat. Yet it goes on, in

sequences of determined investigation.

Segment after segment whenever I
drift in a half-sleep at the
   New Music concert — plunking strings,

low marimba doodles.

2

Not a very promising beginning for a poem
A poem written days later of a dream that took place
only intermittently, and really inconsequentially, at a
concert of post-Webern George Crumb music at the
Philadelphia Art Museum I took my reluctant
   13 year old daughter to, and it wasn't really a
vivid dream, more a music-induced state of

reverie, but the two or three times it happened
it was that

ongoing saga, the search for my stolen coat,
    in Russian, no music,

a dream in almost sepia, bronze, blank copper and
the pewter colors of old samovars,
drifting into and out of the dream, and this
poem also which I'm writing at a
    quarter to two a.m. after
a full plus overtime day of work, washing the
    dishes and cleaning the kitchen,

drifting into and out of the poem
when I nearly fall asleep writing it,

finally actually

falling asleep.

3

Part of me wants to
pursue the poem, go into it, get the

coat, come back, wear it,
map it out, make it available

for further use, the territory, the

dream itself, the sequential as well as

anti-chronological nature of
dream segment followed by reality-segment,

my interest and then
sleepy disinterest in the

whole thing, how we are
magnetized forward into such

fascinating pursuits *(Madame Curie at her
radiant test tubes)* and at the same time

weighted down by the seductively
irresistible anvils of sleep.

4

And there's the dream within the poem and
  the poem within the dream, where the
    true coat is, which is
where I want to get it and
  put it on and come out of both
poem and dream
wearing it, it weighing me down in fact with sheer
weightlessness, lighter than air,
  rising happily past the frames set within
    frames leaning up against a
      phantom wall in my

psyche where I go with heavy lids when the
atmosphere is right, in slow
   methodical pursuit of a
nondescript coat trapped
forever within the intractable laws of
   illusion.

5

But, ironically, the more this fictive
   coat gets invoked, from the
     tiniest fragment of a dream at first, the
more substantial it becomes, the more
   amorphous, Proteus-like, shape-changing from
pea coat, to symbolic coat of old embroidery, to
patched cloak of spiritual envelopment and
   honor, bestowed by its
original wearer, then dream-stuff dissolves, we're in
   a timeless stratosphere, starlight
off the rack, one size fits all, rising
up into it from infinitesimal to
   the stretch fabric of the
     galaxies, one

sleeve dragged through into this world, one sleeve to
   wipe our real mouth with, one
     delicious fuzzy sleeve like the
velvet footpads of my first Teddy-bear whose
silky softness somehow connected me to
   cosmos both

before and after my birth —
   (ah, those velvety feet!).

Coat in which we float forward over
rooftops, past Eiffel Tower and gray
   light of watery dawn, out to

sea, sail of Gargantua, ship of
flight from the confines of this world to what has
never been before until that
coat was assumed by the physical body and
buttoned against foul weather. Collar

open. Long sleeves
   flapping. Coattails
      brushing substantial
      sun-rays. Coat of

emptiness
filled with God's
Breath!

Coat of death

beyond death.

3/30

THE BALLAD OF ROSALEE

I head out across the river
in a skiff of briny skulls

with the full moon as my Klieg light
and twin mice as gondoliers.

The shame pursues my halberd,
I shot the mayor's son,

because of Rosalee,
the baker's daughter.

The bread she baked was ransom
for all the girls of court,

they sang on key for twenty bars
and then fell silent.

I plow the waves with fury,
my public life is o'er.

I'll go into the mountains
as mad as October rain.

I'll fall upon the open fields
and sod-roof houses, farms,

until I flow into the ocean

of my Rosalee's long arms.

I'll fall in drops on tidal waves
I'll pour my water down.

Go back in time, my pretty ones,
go back into the germ

of your conception.

Nothing here of interest,
complications, death.

It's time to hoist your sail, man,
and regulate your breath

so blue rays feast on space there
between the high tide's rush

and receding waves mark everything
that waits for nothing much.

THE SLOW WINGBEAT OF BUTTERFLIES

for Grace Jeschke

1

We gaze down a tube of intensity to find
   what we're looking for, we
     hunch forward with all our
well-fed molecules hunching forward simultaneously
in order to address a letter long overdue,
outfit three ships to set sail for China or
calculate the distant rhomboids of
    ecstatic galaxies,

we gaze down this narrow gauge
glass cylinder of mental concentration in order to
fill out tax forms, subscribe to
   a Rap magazine, untie our
     knotted shoelaces in a
       silent fury at the tight-fisted
cantankerousness of matter and the
intractability of gravity,

and if this tube of hyperspace were used
to project our desires into star-cluster wisdom-nets

what couldn't we expect to discover or
how could we not imagine we'd
   establish ourselves in

    the shadows and lights of God's
innermost courtyards, parquets of four-dimensional
black and white checkerboard tiles
where small roses shower down continuously
and worlds in sharp focus unroll
   constantly into view with absolutely
no more effort on our part
than it takes to breathe out or
say, in a voice suddenly modulated as quietly as
possible,
        "*Ah!*"

2

The endless irony being
   that after our every effort for
     spiritual progress, for energizing ourselves to
make every possible effort at being awake
there's the slow wingbeat of butterflies, how they
   seem to be actually floating in air
with only the most nonchalant effort at
   flying, perhaps they aren't
     flying, but falling and only
    flapping their wings nonchalantly to
       slow their fall,

as perhaps we could do in our walking, putting one
foot out in front of the other to
   just keep from falling,
as Alan Watts said so many years ago at the

Family Dog *Holy Man Jam* in San Francisco late 1960s,

and last Sunday we found ourselves in the 1990s in the
room in the Natural History Museum where they'd put
   hundreds of cocoons
and they hatched and the room
was filled with the
   slow wingbeat of butterflies, zebra-striped and
gossamer white and golden, crossing each other's
   paths, alighting and taking off
so gently, and the

irony is that we make stupendous efforts
only to find that the effortless path often
   leads us to the
greatest of cosmic acknowledgment,
   seismic response,
that we suddenly see the
source and goal of all sunlight, when we
stop scrunching our faces into a ball of
   intense looking and just

circulate among existing circular currents,
buoyed on airwaves,
sitting in our pliable skins around the
   shiny white tree of our
     skeletons, somehow

at the speed and meandering Taoism of the
   slow but gradual wingbeat of butterflies,

letting ourselves bridge each awful yawn of space
with a few flicks of wing-motion, alighting and
　　taking off, with that

same slow effortless butterfly
　　lightness of being.

　　　　　　　　　　　　　　　　　　　　4/11

POEM WRITTEN DURING THE INTERVIEW BY CHARLIE ROSE OF ROBERT MCNAMARA APRIL 19, 1995, IN WHICH MCNAMARA STATES THAT THE VIETNAM WAR WAS WRONG

A porcupine sits on a hill and gazes wistfully over
an ash pile of bones and hair.

A skull with a few combed back strands of hair
sits on a stick and grins a tight wooden grin.

A sky of stretched skin full of empty words and
sterilized corpses sags like a canvas sail
empty of wind.

"There was such a lack of candor about the war."
David Halberstam. "Vietnam is our second
Civil War." David Halberstam.

A black horse rears up on its back legs.

"Total lack of candor."

I want to fly a thousand luminous ribbons
over the graves of each of the slain.

I want to boil a tin of butter and cinnamon
on the graves of each of the slain.

I want to draw a moustache of green lichen on

the upper lip of the skull of each of the slain.

I want to dip the sun of life into each eye socket
where a blue porcupine
sits on a hill surrounded by
sulfurous smoke.

What wall couldn't we knock down then
that stands today in Washington D.C. inscribed with
the names of the American slain,
not the Vietnamese slain, that wall
would be too long and costly to
erect in their honor.

What wall of reinforced concrete and steel
wouldn't give way to the pressure of our very
human bodies all pushing against it day and
night to no avail?

What would have convinced the McNamaras and
Kennedys and Johnsons and Westmorelands of the
world that people were dying wretched deaths in
tropical mud to no avail?

What madness prevailed?

4/19

PREPARATIONS FOR SLEEP

1

I knew a man who before he went to
  bed draped himself in
    lion skin with lion headdress
      flowing golden mane he'd
arrange just so on the pillow, purring as he
drifted off to sleep. I knew a

woman would wind herself in
  yellow silk, insert her
    fingers into huge fake rings of
Spanish Contessa jewels to flash and
dazzle the darkness she drew around her like a tent to
float forward horizontally into sleep. I knew

a couple who would carefully dress each other in
Pharaonic loincloths and shirts of hieroglyphics and
fringes of corn tassels
so they'd go hieratically vertical in
    two-dimensional emblematic
  immortality, in profile, into
sleep.

Sleep the mystery. Sleep the dark blank with
  fast and furious cartoons of
    essential surreality, re-
imagining the imagination soup of our

hours and actions walking around by day in
    quote reality unquote, wearing the
clothes of our offices, the official uniforms of our
stations, slyly concealing the

hair shirts and pinky brown skintight suits of our
bodily adornments just before
    slipping off into dream,

ready in the finery of our most fertile thoughts
to speed down the runway of possible
    mortality and head up into
        slide-back after slide-back of
    purest blue sky

into true space and true time,
dropping a real diamond onto the
    ground as lasting
      shadow of our
sudden takeoff, letting a cloud instead

wave goodbye to the
    fond groundlings.

2

Another prepared for sleep by shrugging off all
vestiges of the world, he stood up
and buildings slid onto the floor, famine and
    war, flood and individual despair

fluttered down from his shoulders like
    dry newspapers,
he dislodged ditches of blood as well as
    rainbows above yellow meadows, he
discarded blown-out tanks filled with
    surprised youths in
        blackened bodies as well as
first flushes of adolescent Eros, sweet
    golden-haired tinges of peach sweetness
also drifting off him like
    echoing melody, down to

essential nakedness more
ultimately bare than the bare body,
more naked than unfrozen waterfalls down
    mile-high cliffs in
      virgin territory bathed in
        perpetual mist,
more naked than the roil of volcanic gush down
mountainsides, more naked than
the naked eye that
glances at all this with
    infant innocence,

he divests himself of history and time
until, inside out to this world, even

future events are vacuumed into
    bliss.

Then he sleeps.

                                              5/2

EVERYONE AT THE MALL

If I could sit long enough in the
   food arcade of this
     downtown mall, watching all these

human beings pass and repass, pass by so
intently or nonchalantly beamed in on
   being themselves completely

I think I could plumb the depths of the mystery of the
monstrosity of Genghis Khan as well as
the saintliness of Saint Theresa,

it's all here in
gleam of eye, smile of lip, crease of brow,
furtive suspicious glance, laugh of gladness,
sweetness, sinister secretiveness,

darkness,
light.

5/10

THE MAN WITH ONE EYE

If a man with one eye in the absolute
   middle of his forehead
should accost you and ask you just
what in the world you think you are doing,
what in the world with its fiery ribbons of
   feeling and half-articulated thoughts,
what in the world that keeps coming together like
   cube-shaped molecules to form a
   flashy momentary pattern before
     jigsawing away into a

billion disparate pieces again
equally flashy, takes a tiny gnat's breath
then begins again its colossally interconnecting of
atoms and mustaches, wagging tongues and
   wagging tails, diamonds on pedestals in
     high Andean caves, a small perfect
pearl of drool on a
   Newton's lip,

just what in this world of bone-like scaffolds and
folding paper fans,
just what in this world you are doing!

Reply in a series of equally atomic non-sequiturs,
batting your eyelashes at the rate of
   skaters across still green forest ponds and
pointing your right index finger upward at cloudy nothing:

"All beauty is skin deep,"
"I never met a man I didn't like,"
"Your silver bicycles of memory are stacked against
 a barn wall in blazing sunlight,"
"A fly buzzed when I died,"
"The tortured wonder when it will be over,
the torturers when it will begin,"

and smile as whole cities go over the rapids in a
 spray of mile-high mist and
  twinkling lights,
millenniums stutter by slowly as on rickshaws of lace,
faces turn in an absinthe light and
 articulate these sentences on slow-motion lips,
green glow pervasive as dust,
the nighttime coming on,
solitaries beginning their long walks down
 long solitudinous streets,
the moon striking one.

And if this man with his one eye in the
 absolute middle of his forehead
is dissatisfied with your answers
try leaping through the air with the clenched
 jaws of a jaguar, yellow slant-eyes beaming,
or try sitting deathly still for just one second and notice
that the world continues like clockwork but its
face has burst into blue incandescence, its words accelerated
 beyond all reasonable speed.

He'll rub his one eye in disbelief.

His one eye will grow drowsy.

His face will grow as long as a spaniel's.

His heart will open his other eye.

5/16

THE OCEAN OF LOVE

1

"I want to descend the successive oceans of love"
   he said, and
drank a thimble of dew.

*"I want to scale the windy horrendous heights of
divine madness,"* he proclaimed,
and stood on a stepladder waving his arms.

*"I want to achieve greatness, depth, width and length and
  harness the elegant zigzags of power,"* he
    intoned, nibbling the nib of his
      ballpoint pen as
    mud splashed his cuffs.

When in the depths of the ocean of love let the
bathysphere door open, the fish flood in with their
curious fixed glances, and drown.

When the peak of divine madness is in sight and your
    legs have snapped off at the knees
the last miles will be golden, each brick
   outlined in your own DNA
     singing back to you
       meteorological heights and
  angelic articulations.

As for the length and breadth of greatness, the
    moth knows the
  greatest greatness as it
      incinerates in flame, all
ideas of itself forgotten in the molten moment of its
desire's apotheosis, only flame left, not even
    dusty traces of moth wing or
       thorax, wiggling antennae or mandible,
only the flick of a flicker of flame and a

snap back to straight burning.

2

The shoes we have for such travel are made of scrolls.
The umbrella to keep out acid rain
is our own skin stretched on our own
      slim ribs of bone.

Ha! The madman sings of love
    at the bottom of the sea, salt in his eyes.

The lover sings at top voice on Annapurna peaks
and the echo itself swallows him alive, the
   echo alone comes down from the
mountaintop stark naked, as beautiful as
   Adonis, as splendid as a
           Swiss morning.

The great one walks with an ant's shadow,

casts an ant's shadow against the wall,
thinks ant thoughts, carries out burdens
light as feathers

      great distances.

3

What can be said about the oceans of love
are windows so huge black velvet
drapes of entire night hang like
    postage stamps in their frames,
all planets and all stars twinkle like
tiny lights on the surface of its lake,
the entire speech of it so lengthy and
   varied that one word becomes a
world that comes into being, evolves and
dies out into the first blink that bore it
before it can link with another word
   to form a
      single sentence.

Ah, the oceans of love!
What clandestine embraces, porpoise and
    mudlark, platypus and
muskrat and their instinctive infatuations,
making a grand wheel that goes
   around and around against the
     noisy night, the chain of
being, each eye focused ahead, each

 eyebeam reciprocated even
  shyly by someone as eager to

love as to be loved!

4

 I've already said a lot of nothing about the
  oceans of love, not even the
   first twitch of eyelash
    accurately recorded
much less the amazing blue mist that
hovers over a Minnesota
  cornfield and orange heat rays
   flash down to ignite the
barn but bring in a golden harvest
  for the first time in forty years.

There's no measurement to God's compassion,
one percent of which is in this world, ninety-nine
  in the next —
mouse shouts wriggling in
  anticipation of their mother's return
in a tiny niche behind the hay loft
or the ducks' parade past overall'd
   workers by their plows
or the bumblebees' orchestra of cellos on a
  summer afternoon —

don't begin to reflect the full measure of

love's gorgeous pouring so
    plentifully down and through every
sentient creature intent on spending that
portion of divine love down to the last
air bubble popping on deathbed lips pursed to
    kiss cloud and sand dune
        hello and goodbye at the
    same time, the great wave
reared up on its water drops back a
    hundred miles in absolute
suspended animation, each drop held in
timeless suspension as a
    whole world is reflected on its
        perfect oblong sphere
of car wreck with spirit essences magnetically
drawn upward by the power of divine love,

of fresh garden with dew lacquered green grass blades
onto which two medieval peasants fling themselves
    down into the spinning vortex of
        divine love,

of a scroll unrolled across Chinese temple floor,
    mirror polished teak, depicting amid
    ink-splashed smoke and rapid strokes
armies in furious battle drawn together by the
flip side of divine love, which, at the
    moment of mortality in combat, shows its
    unbearably beautiful almost geometric
        perfection as a golden sword of
pure light penetrates a warrior's heart and comes out

somewhere in a fountain in Paradise to the
relieved shock of the wounded spirit in his
    blood-speckled bamboo armor —

the great wave of the ocean of love holds its
frothy head high in a pellucid blue sky as
tick after tick on the sprocketed film of
divine love flicks by revealing stolen glimpses of
moments in each of our lives, the most
  wretched among us, when for a
    split second the
cricket of love's messenger rubs legs against
thorax to chirr the telegram of direct speech of love
onto the drenched heart of the beloved

and stones all around start to glisten,
flame bends frantically to listen,
sky clears to a point of utter transparency

as life passes through thick
layer after layer in the
ocean of love
and hits bottom, gives up, submits,
  lays down its
arms,

and the wave resumes its crash course to
conclusion and pours all those
world-pictures down onto the singlemost
person awaiting love's desperate reply,
moistened inwardly from head to foot

in that ocean we all feel in the
arm and neck ache and burning eyes and
    dry tongue

of love's delicious ocean

beating so rhythmically against our

magnesium shore.

5/16-21

PALACE IN THE TREETOPS

As I came out of the bookstore I
glanced up at the treetops and there was a
green palace built there and the
   golden tinge of sunlight was
     confined to illuminating it
more than the lightly tossing foliage of the tree.

It was vagrant, made of nothing,
calling the dormant mind awake as if to
   glass flute music and the
    calls across space of
     self-identifying birds,

insubstantial ivory of air, carved latticework more
intricate than leaf veins under microscopes,

the palace no one inhabits, tossing on the
   treetops, lit golden and
   rosy by late sunglow,

to which I turn now in writing this,
pulled as well as held from and in my mortal
   place on the ground actually
unable to just float up to where my
imagination of splendor would go, although
this in itself should be sufficient enough,

this meager essay in spatiality

and the fugitive vision
and our capacity and love for the
   fabulous and our

intransigent right to be there.

5/22

ANCIENT ZIGGURAT

The ancient ziggurat stairs to God are filled with
   ghostly impediments to
      unimpeded ascent. First there's this
bodily physique like an old well you drop a creaky bucket down
 at night
to draw up some cold fresh water in the blue
   moonlight but it
comes up drier and drier each day, so the
   old folks say,
(but I say — one green grass blade springing in the air is
   worth all your
well-running high-tech state of the art factories producing
     hundreds of tons of the
  Gross National Product per day!)

Then there's the
no air zone, the no ozone zone, the no zebras on the
   highway after 10p.m zone, the no
    smoking, no spitting, no hugging zones
running like an equator around the
planet of material shapes, turning us all into
   rainforest lunchbreaks in which one live
     edible something is worth all the
   swamp crocodiles you can muster.
Matter in jigsaw configuration, four dimensional and
   then some! Cascades of brittle
     geometry going straight up for miles
interposing ghostly skyscrapers between

us and the Infinite, obscuring that moonlike
    smile slanting down…

Then there's all the complex manifestations of time,
time past we longingly search for like
   health-addict Prousts hunting the
     grail of eternal youth, or there's
the heady nostalgia felt behind every breath
for the present moment right smack in the middle of that
very present moment, a nanosecond of
   mortal grief making an
     interplanetary gulf in what otherwise would be
standing at a railing overlooking the Grand Canyon and
enjoying the russets and mauve purples oozing their
   snaky light up the
     distant gullies and ravines —

Then, as we struggle our pitiful way
   closer to the top, over massed
     shapes in clumps, bodies of past
actions pulling moth-eaten blankets around
   bony shoulders against the
     frost, as we get

closer and closer to the top we see that the
biggest impediment on the ancient ziggurat
is the cavernous hollows of our selves, the
   repetitive ins and outs, cries for
help to the wrong lifeguard, the one with
his bathing suit backwards and a fiery monocle,
in which we do not dive so deep down into

   our shivering selves that the
raw pieces implode, but
lounge in limited definitions of what a
    glorious thing it is
      to be human,
poppy in one hand, blank book in the
other, hat pulled
  down over the
    eyes,

a poignant reminder of the end
in a tender moment suspended on a hair

between grudging submission
and relief.

                                                  5/26

BAD STANZAS

I had to cross a few bad stanzas out
and it was like drawing a white glove across
   a face become pale with grief,
a moment so earnestly felt and so
   carefully worded into images of
     nearly tropical color
crossed out,

dropped down the Chute of Forgetfulness,
made to be as if they were not, never existed,

verbal weeds in a fertile bed ripped out to
  make way for
    new growth when tomorrow's
      sunlight hits. It was like
a wide patch of snow had covered the evidence,
the wrench and pistol on the
glass night table were
  quickly dispatched into the plant, which,
    luckily, had large noisy leaves.

Those stanzas in all their clumsy innocence were like
interplanetary bugs on a platform about to
launch into space, time-travel forward and all,
  but they had to be
swept off with one swoop and now
flit over garbage dumps, lost among refuse, bedraggled,
    crossed out,

their presence in the universe reversed,
their gaiety hushed, not even funereal, no
   black bunting draped across the ends of their
      direct objects or verbs, no bouquets of
lovely tropes in horseshoe-shapes by an open
coffin, not even cremation,

but lines drawn through them like
innocent citizens on an assassin's list,
   disappeared, never mentioned
       again.

Based on their essential
badness? Inconsequential noodling?
Wasting all our precious time? Taking up
   precious space on the page? No-counts?
Metrically inappropriate? Off track?

How they got there in the first place
   nobody knows. Bloodless? Anemic? Gaseous?
(I probably dozed off mid-stanza.)
How they stayed so long nobody can explain.
They didn't keep things
   moving? Showed no
special wit? Illuminated no
hidden corners or nooks?

Ah, why am I going on and on about two or three
dispensable stanzas? Out of fear for the
   worth of the whole?

If two stanzas are
judiciously but ruthlessly discarded, where will it
 end?

Will I be left with
one word or image worth saving?

Will my own self be
x-d out in the process?

Will nothing be left
where I worked so long and hard —

 but blank pages?

5/27

AT SEA

1

If you were cast into the sea but a word could be a
life raft to take you to safety
   what would that word be?

The elephants of the intellect
   lumber away from the scene.
Heart-shaped lights in loopy strings
   reflect in the water.

"Well," says the realist, *"for me
the word would be: Survival!"*

"Nice choice," says Mr. Lexicon with his
   pince-nez nicely perched.

The romantic weighs in: *"Love,"* he says,
   drawing out the o-v-e of the word as if it were
a long wooly glove he was pushing his
fingers in all the way to the tips.

"Such a word might leave you high and dry,"
said the cynic who'd been around, who'd
   seen a thing or two.

"Then what would your word be," Mrs.
Diligent Punctilious shot pointedly at the cynic.

"Why, no word at all, of course," he
intoned, a bit too like
brushed felt, his face turning to walnut.

A very small man whose shadow was
   bigger than he was
said the word that would save us all,

took a run at it and
leapt into it and it

headed out to the high seas where it
tossed him overboard and he sank to the
pearl-lined bottom lost in translucence

with the Divine Name of Allah

glowing on his lips and
silver fish licking at his heels.

2

Of course the word most auspicious
and most efficacious is the one
most pronounceable of the most
   unpronounceable word that
engulfs even the most intractable
   to its lips.

Take *"forever"* for example, its

forefront *"for"* sitting like a locomotive
   steaming down the tracks, a
head of steam and iron
determination, and its caboose, *"ever,"*
energetic, supplying to *"for"* its nuggets of
     power. Or take

"evanescence." There's a word for the squeamish!
You say it and already it
   starts to inflate.

"Lackadaisical" is another one full of
   floatable oxygen, but it
   doesn't have helicopter
     liftability over
   expanses of water.
For that we need the word that made its
   first speaker's lips golden,
that, once spoken, opened skies as if they were
   drapery. That showed
   clouds like stairways over
     the treacherous canyons of
   ourselves whose
deeps can lead to our own
self-imposed destruction.

"Say Allah! And you will see wonders,"
said Moroccan master, Shaykh Darqawi, and we
attest to that, verify its authenticity and
   its truth.
Even the high seas themselves become

   satisfactorily diminished to fit into that
word's sweet vowel sounds like two
     tear drops of salt water.

Gulls fly overhead, islands float into view,
happy faces of islanders
   celebrating its
     fiery pronouncement.

The flames of it rise to the
   lower heavens, the dancers around it
cast shadows on the highest hills.
Whoever pronounces it is
   safe from burning.
It encompasses every existent from
atomic fingersnap of Big Bang to
   last suck-in of breath at the end
as well as the arch of continuous white
   bird flight between those two
moments made visible by the

pronunciation of that word, providing
comfort to us all.

3

Word passed between the lips of angels
   like incandescent blue hoops with
     tiny wings all around it fluttering on its
       own,

word like a lumbering tank made of giant armor
   plates with rivets as big as fire hydrants
crushing the skeletons of protestors
    in Freedom Square on a Spring afternoon,

word that once uttered becomes
    opposite to what it was, becomes
       latticework of sorrows that sounded as
happy as a New Orleans brass band on a
    barge going down the levee,

word looming hauntedly like a medieval cathedral
with a chattering of ancient words trapped
   inside ricocheting from one
     mausoleum to another in the
   gray winter mist,

word of scientific precision that isolates
one particular microscopic cilia from
    another in a segment of bacteria
     moving across a dish of liquid
       like a dragon caught in Jello,

words that transform themselves from
    butterfly to lead pencil, from
     kaleidoscope to cascade, from
River Nile to nihilism, opium to
    operating room, Romanian to
roar of lion which bounces across a
proprietary portion of the forest and comes back to
the roarer with grammatically correct echo,

  gratifying the old beast's ears so that he may
lie down and nap in peace that his
  kingdom is intact,

word that wins a kingdom, word that loses one,
word that hovers above and one that
  sinks to the bottom,
word that sinks us to our knees, and one that
stands us up ready for battle,

made of one part air and one part sound,
aether and ectoplasm, with a portion of the
object of the idea it represents
  imbedded invisibly in it like a
   sliver of the true cross in a
   frame of sanctified silver,

word which when pronounced provides us these
bodies from marrow outward, clothes us with
  flexible flesh and mouths
and glottises capable of
  continuing the sentence of our
  creation to the end,

word of light blinking on and
  enlightening the silence of its
ultimate context,

word of the living
  pronounced over the
mute pronunciation of the dead,

word that comes full circle
passed between the lips of angels
like incandescent blue hoops with
tiny wings all round it fluttering
       on their own.

LOOKOUT / an interlude

I'm building a lookout in the branches of the
   highest tree available
in hopes of catching God's movements against the
nuclear curtain of the sky,
putting ivory latticework from the tomb of the Taj Mahal
knitted together with raw palm plaiting from
   Borneo, brush-grass raffia-work mixed with
Moroccan inlay of finest tiniest mother of pearl
   triangles,
the complete set of Don Quixote volumes as
   translated by Tobias Smollet in
   suitable antiquated case,
cobbled together with sacred texts from every
   revelation, pages of parchment
     pasted with dove's blood,

Ah, the lookout platform sways and almost
   hurls me down,
the tree sustains me with its thick gnarled
   aorta-like tubular trunk
flexible as breathing,
and I gaze out over America and the world,

press my face against the coolness of the
   starry sky, I've brought my

pens and notebook all the way up here with me
to jot down the hectic dots and dashes of
   godly dictation, hand
      whirring like a propeller,
heart as hushed as a choirboy waiting for his cue,
body as still as a desert as it's
   about to slip unnoticed under the
      thick door of night

and as I listen for the proper words
I lean forward a little —

I lean forward
   just a little.

———————————————

4

One word's a tree, look how it's
   grown and split into prefix and suffix enough
for a family of small verbs with
   pale blue shells to live in,

one word's the affection between
Coffee the young cat and my peculiar human person
   which she just now wishes to
      demonstrate as I try writing this

poem, including lovingly gnawing my
    fountain pen as I write, me having to
stop to stroke her face as she closes her
    eyes in pleasurable acknowledgment as well as
    shoo her away so the
        spell won't get broken,

another word's the calamitous
train crash underground with its
    scream of brakes and rails, sparks in
hissing spray, huge clank of
    cars against each other and
    blackout,

another word's the sublime painless deliverance from
the tragedy in the form of troops of lateral
    angels shouldering the
    burden of souls heavenward

(the cat's back, cold nose
    brushing my elbow) —

all the words of life strung infinitely out on their
own genetic strings across the
    abyss of wordlessness that is both
        deep and dragon-dark with its
        deafening silence as well as,
flipped over, light with ebullience and
    mute sunshine, core of the
        word-world spinning like a
            billion suns,

and we float our hushed speech over that abyss
and dance at its fiesta,

we fling from our depths to the equally
   dark depths of space
words God's given us to bridge the
   inarticulate with feeble song,
     over which processions of caribou
       wary of hunters
cross into Alaskas of eternal night
in search of fresh lichen and
   the illuminations of the
       Northern Lights

before which no tongue can fashion
anything to resemble them
but go dry then moist

with the essential God-given
vocabulary of humanity,

eyes wide with wonder.

                                          5/31-6/7

SHAKE THE BOX

When you shake the box right up to your ear
it rattles, there's the
sound of an accordion unwheezing,
the sound of a factory building being reduced to rubble
with the cries of its million workers
   unstifled after fifty years,

the sound of one drop of water hitting porcelain.

If you turn the box and shake it
you might hear Imhotep's great
   oration at the
     opening of the pyramid,
the Psalms sung in their original voice with
original accompaniment of deft harp-plucks, original
echoes repeated by the
   mountains and finally
     handed on to the angels to
repeat to infinity in their domain.

Shake the box, the "music" begins, the
creaking of distant doors,
the doors that swung open to reveal
Salomé weeping at the deed she had done,
the strange rumbling of door
   opening on strange hunchbacked
Genghis Khan plotting his next invasion
by sputtering pig-fat candle over unrolled sheepskin maps on

   teak tables,
and you might see the gleam in his eye
or hear the downfall in his voice, a
    guttural subtext to his
       bravery that betrays him.

This box once shaken
reveals aspects never before known
like the dark side of the moon once was,
such as the actual identity of Shakespeare,
his daily personality and the look on his face as he
    wrote those plays,
the actual murderer of Kennedy with all the
    events and shady dealings leading up to it,

all things just within reach and just out of reach,
this little box full of galaxies
that resounds in its deepest silences
with God's own silences, in its
divine creakings
with God's utterances,

and in it there's the whispering
   push out of stem from delicate seedling,
hissing larval intensities as transformations ensue,
pop of gradual or sudden planet-birth or
pop of star-annihilation across
   fiery distances into a Black Hole's
super-cool tactile immediacies,
soothing voice in space articulated like the strutwork of a
   complicated Utopia built with subatomic structures,

a sound as silent as the tomb
from which no fax has yet been received
at our all-too human station.

Shake the box.
You'll hear nothing.

Shake it again
and you'll hear angels sigh

inside that nothing.

                                                                6/8 (5a.m.)

AW, GO TO SLEEP

for Paul Grillo

Tonight I'm just going to pull back the covers,
   climb in and go to sleep.

I'm not going to get one of my million unread
   books and try to read it, or
      even try to write the
         greatest poem ever written,
I'm just going to go to sleep. What a luxury!

I'm not going to think about the
   situation of the world, why
      God created wickedness and how He
   uses it to temper our
      intemperate souls,
I'm just going to go to bed and go to sleep.

I'm not going to worry about why
Allen Ginsberg doesn't like my poetry, or
   why I don't win those big
      poetry prizes.
I'm just going to lie down on my right side and
   drift right off into
      unconsciousness.

Not think of Moroccan back alleys adrift in the
   sweet scent of cedar wood,

nor visualize coppery Nigerian sunsets.
Just sleep. No epiphanies, no
   rhapsodies, just sleep.

I'm not going to formulate in my mind the epic sweep of
imagery possible in the lyric, the
  meaningful juxtapositions of
    erotic and spiritual elements which are so
poignantly human,
  exciting an idea as it is. I'm too tired.
I'm just going to go to sleep. Tonight, exhausted,
just sleep.

Not worry about moments of devotion slipping by
    un-devoted, nor
  whether this high, dark, impassible rock heart of mine
will ever really budge and fall
  down to let
    waters of wisdom gush out and
      wash out these years of
well-intentioned error,
and even now I'm letting it get away from me.
I'm going to resist it. I'm
turning in to just
  sleep. I'm

not even going to go over familiar territory,
  evoke Napoleon, Alexander the Great,
    Harpo Marx.
Just close these fried eyes and
   sleep. I'm tired.

All the thoughts that need to be thought
  before I die, snip them off and let them
    float,
all the illuminations of those who have
   gone before providing
     stepping stones of light for us to
       kneel on in our
journey, exerting ourselves like
bands of steel pulling huge pistons.
Not tonight, I'm going
right to sleep. The
  engine wheels are
    bearing down. My wristwatch says
2 a.m. again, night after night, when
owls are on the wing and
   hookers weep and the
   cold streets sleep,
I'm going to sleep.

Without building a pyramid of words, without
   taming the ostrich of my
     clandestine desires,
without moving a finger to do so,
without puzzling out a solution to the
   problems of the world which could be
     solved in an instant of
gold powder falling through a beam a light
   spelling out every
     human utterance ever uttered,

but I can't write them all down tonight as I

usually do. Tonight I'm going to
resist the temptation.

I'm just going,
without ceremony or strain,
to sleep.

There.
I'm asleep.

6/14

COSMIC PARADOX

The torturer stopped his torturing just long enough to
stand back, and in the time it takes to
   light a cigarette or
      pull a lever
an abyss opened up in the air between
him and his victim
and he was in it, encoiled in an embrace of angels
   that spanned every known horizon.

The rapist stopped to catch his breath
   from so much hammering
and a thousand angels on a steep incline
reached down to surround him with the
    electrical charge he longed for, and the
   bodily release.

The hatchet murderer stopped swinging...
but this poem's become predictable.
What isn't predictable is that
the saintly almsgiver paused with coin-filled hand in
   midair just long enough for the
     brackish cackles of hell to echo up and
       wash around his ineluctable gesture.

The genius heart surgeon paused with scalpel in hand
just long enough for
   sudden devouring flames to
flash through him as if he were an

    old wooden house full of
       perishable memories.

Something in a moment between the clicks of the living,
a pause so short it wouldn't show up on any
    measuring device except perhaps
the slow fall of an oblong waterdrop from a
spout to the drain in a sink
or the glisten in a tear and the sudden
    appearance of that tear without warning on an
       otherwise dispassionate cheek.

Here we have skies full of concerned angels
throwing ropes of grace to perpetrators of
       horror. We have
hellishs gorges and jagged fissures opening up sideways
in otherwise beneficent and saintly occurrences.

Even this poem itself which came unannounced
at a quarter to two on a June evening while
brushing my teeth, and suddenly I'm not in my
    small bathroom but in a
       plain barracks out in an empty quarter
where the tortured won't wake the neighbors nor
    disturb the sleep of journalists or priests,

or out in thick forests way past the last habitations
where the rape victims' sobs won't
    startle the farmers, although in
       some cases the farmers are their fathers
made to watch the brutal decapitation of honor

as the vicious animality of an
   otherwise rather religious and
      cleancut soldier turns him into a
Behemoth roaring up from the deep
   ocean of the ground under our feet
and chains of thousands of years of pain
are secured firmly around the ankles of the
   girl shot forward from puberty to
      a widowhood of the human heart,
   widowhood and motherhood
        achieved in the same instant,

but in this infinitesimal moment occurring
inexplicably to the worst examples of inhumanity
black rainbows of efflorescence suddenly
   open like wounds in the inner world of
      all of us at once,

small white birds like pearls with wings fly out on
linked strings across gorges of impossibility
that separate the actor from his act,
and in a world often unbearable to look at
invisible forces put on momentary masks of the
      utmost sublimity,

a choir snorts, a pig sings an aria,
a volcano sounds like a wind chime,
a rock falls like a downfloating sea horse
through emerald water.

                                                              6/3

DOORKNOB

"Old Mr. Aches & Pains," they called him.
   although he felt about the same otherwise,
had the same thoughts, the same gyroscope for a heart,
   the same merry-go-round dipped in amber inside,
the same iced-over lake in winter
where a blue woman with one giant
   fluttering wing on top of her head
would appear from time to time,

the same crumpled road map with divine yellow
  light like low-lying mist
     playing across it.
Otherwise, he was getting old. Yup.
Creaky, dippy, sleepy, chirpy, flatulent, quirky,

he fled along the smoke trails,
he swam the choppy seas,

his eyelids felt like heavy weights,
he felt less like an immortal god, thank God!

His teeth looked great in a glass!
The mirror showed an old cypress
  with a benevolent smile.
    Bending forward.
      Shedding leaves.

He had one hand

   on the doorknob of death.

He wore golden shoes.

When he laid his body down
   in the velvet case
the hinges squeaked as he
     closed the lid.

Like an old tooth brush, now he was free!

He roamed at will.

He saw with a round eye.

                                              6/24

SEVEN SHORT FABLES

There were seven serpents and the man had to
walk among them. They were
   his own soul protecting him and
     killing him.

There was a giant ghost ship that loomed up in the
   night. The captain was dead. The crew were
     dead. The ocean was the
       heart of despair.

Twelve rocks sang in chorus. Twelve birds
   landed on them, one by one.
The birds listened. The rocks sang.
The world was one.

One day an old lady said to the air, *"Be
clear for me!"* It
opened up and tall dark angels came down
and led her up glass stairs.

Once upon a time a window looked back at
someone looking out of it, and smiled.
The person looking out of it wept.

Thus the world goes around.

Once there was a world. It swung to and fro
   in space. Half was in light

Half in darkness. Most of the
   people in the light were awake.
Most of the people in the darkness
   were asleep.

Once there was a dragon who ate butterflies.
One particularly gorgeous butterfly, morpho blue,
wide wingspread, about to be swallowed into his
fiery maw, cried out
"No god but God!"
and the dragon became a young man
sitting by a waterfall

watching butterflies.

7/4

A VERY SHORT POEM

We are these self-propelled beings.

That in itself is dangerous.

7/4

EIGHT SHORT LIFE STORIES

Mr. Chernofsky bought a Pekinese at the
  age of ninety-three, and fed it a
    constant diet of cheese crackers
      until he died.

Parbub Mahalaila wore a long green
  dress at her wedding, and
wore the same dress at the wedding of her
  nine children in the village clearing known as
"Pumpkin Glen," and at the baptism of her grandchildren.

Tör Rodmüssen began a life of penmanship after
  he had given up fishing. His hands were
gnarled but his will to perfection in the
  art of making letters was strong, and slowly
    perfection prevailed.

Thab Musmusmus spoke only the truth, and then
  only when asked.

Glandular problems arose in the later years of
Margaret Spitz and she could only get about
  with difficulty, although she still
    loved to gaze at the seven cornfields.

Hector Valle Mendoza Carlión grew up on the ocean and lived
on the ocean and died on the ocean
  holding a frayed piece of rope.

Mrs. Kuan Chang ate candied ginger every day of
her life just after 3 o'clock, and
    flipped through the family photo album
        every night just after seven.

Left to his own devices
Malfred Droog, at 14, was no harm to anyone, and
    actually had the
        power to heal.

                                                                                          7/5

RAWHIDE FIGURE

If that thing, that feeling, that
   trembling of our absolute essence we
experienced, combination of love and lust,
intellectual, soul-shaking, that we felt
towards certain people in our past, perhaps now lost, at the

time we were hopelessly attracted to, even attained
that totality of infatuation with them, it was
reciprocated, we were
   willing to almost die for them in a rush of
     feeling, we felt
happily burned alive anyway and their
physical and pheromenal perfume was
so potent we were literally made
other-than-ourselves,

I'm talking an ego-less
passion here, fecund, luxurious, towards
one or two people in our lives to that intensity,
perhaps experienced even now to our own present
   wives or husbands,

somehow if that state or whatever it was were personified
would the figure or charm
even be human? Would it be a
small, say, rawhide figure of a
person, or might it be instead
part human part deer, with antlers,

a golden halo'd personification of an
earthly and celestial force in
   nature, shamanistic,
charm-like, pot of
gold that is also a boiling honey pot,
    balm or resin
caught at the edge of an arctic tundra
wild beasts go in search of, dolphins and
    whales miles undersea
       naturally manufacture, it's a

deep secretion from a secret
mechanism in the universe, it
glows and pulsates from some distant
   star or planet, it's
revealed after severe earthquake in a
deep rift in the earth laid bare like a fleshly nugget
capable of serene fever bringing sweet
   delirium to its victims,

a kind of dancer, wispish as
blue flame, darting into the
center and circling around our circumference
      simultaneously,

flame with a face of utter loveliness that
looks at us with nearly delirious
topaz eyes, eyes you could
   float horizontally into for
miles,
flaming iceberg, suspended,

transported, potent dimensionless
creature akin to fairies, burnished
as teak, dark, sultry with purplish
lips like lips that have just sucked blackberries,

sexual but intellectual savor, spiritual
   whirlwind with recognizable human
      personality, love-magnet,

inspirer of a glorious sanity maybe only
once in our lives, maybe lasting forever, leaves us
   transformed, fused,

emotional, intellectual and physical
luminosity
made into
one whole being

suspended in space
like a star.

                              7/2

SILVER WATER FROM A SPOUT

I want to grow old as colorfully
   as possible,
I don't want to be a bald and blank old man
pale as a faded envelope, limp and used up
    like an old dollar bill.
I want green eyebrows and rosy cheeks
and baggy trousers and shoes that
   curl up at the ends.

I might even wear huge paper wings that drag behind me
as my dear wife of fifteen years did from
   time to time on the
     streets of Berkeley in the mid-60's,
once boarding a plane in full regalia to the
uncanny lack of astonishment of her fellow
    passengers.

I don't want to fold together like the covers of an old
   book or end up more like the
    stiff back of the chair I'm in than a
     man, I want to
entertain cosmological notions way into my
90's and still perambulate peripatetically between
   equally noble cypress trees
    overlooking a turquoise sea.

None of us needs to blink into space like
captive zoo animals in old age, the great nautical

  adventures of discovery take place with
contemporary regularity, prows poking out of
  creaking ribcages,
maps spread out across the breathing tables of our lungs
and secret spiritual staircases spotlit with clarity
  winding endlessly up through floor after
    floor of our cervical vertebrae

where we may ascend in the concentrically symmetric
  middle of the night
    to hold elegant conversations with
Herman Melville still tormented by the high seas of doubt,
'Ibn 'Arabi as radiant and vocal as a constellation,
Emily Dickinson as sharp as a head-on collision with
  mortality,
Blake in the midst of an epiphany,
and all the prophets from the Prophet Muhammad (peace be
  upon him) backward to Adam

as at ease in a breeze-blown woods walking between
cypress trees as we are, in old age, those
yearning eyes in the front of our heads
agleam as ever, infinity signs for pupils,
light pouring out of them

like silver water from a spout.

7/7

A PLACE FOR THE NIGHT

Tonight I'm going to sleep on a rock,
  or maybe I'll sleep on a live coal.
Maybe I'll sleep in the middle of the
   stadium where Leni Riefenstahl filmed
Triumph of the Will, and Hitler raised an
  already mummified hand to
    thousands of Nazi youth. I'll
curl up right in the middle of the crowd
and sleep like a baby.

Or maybe I'll sleep in The Last Days of Pompeii,
lava forever, peacefully stoned.
Or on a windowsill overlooking the Civil War.
Peaceful as a flock of birds going south,
   cutting their giant
"V" through the clear blue sky.

I'll sleep the sleep
of the thoroughly innocent, the unblemished,
asleep in the rollers and breakers of the
  Atlantic like a piece of forgotten
   flotsam. Or under the table of the
Nicene Council with scrolls of the rejected gospels,
wriggling my toes among holy manuscripts soon to be
   tossed into flames and
    nearly lost to mankind forever, the
  only eyewitness accounts to the
     Savior of Souls.

Maybe I'll sleep atop the Himalayas, or
be asleep on Macchu Picchu plateau when
Pablo Neruda just reaches the crest and
   reaches for his pen in his breast pocket
      before catching his breath.

Maybe I'll find a little nook at the beginning of the
   world, near some combinant and rapidly
      recombinant atoms, a snore or
   two and I'm shot to the
      end of the 20th century in a
         basket of star debris.
Asleep when the continents shift, the dinosaurs
   come and go leaving their
      silly footprints and
fugitive pieces of themselves to
   tantalize future paleontologists.

When I wake up and rub my eyes
maybe I'll be in the sky itself, suspended as a
      cloud,

raining over Nebraska.

7/10

SWEET COSMOLOGIES

1

Theories of the Universe rolled in through the
   open window and the
sweet madman with lips like white roses
sorted them out and put them into little
    ebony trays. There was the

"Multiple Identical Universes" theory in which
the sweet madman with lips like white roses
was actually a billion identical
sweet madmen with lips like white roses
and his nimble fingers plucked nimble lutes
and rings on his multiple fingers
   multiplied the universes in which he
plucked those lutes as well as
reflected all their rounded reflections
onto a single shield that
   blazed with a singular light.

Then there was the *"Universe As a
Golden Hairpin"* theory, put absent-mindedly into the
    hair of a particularly voluptuous
woman of fair blue skin and pale irises
as she sat on the edge of her gilded divan
   floating on the froth of a
      coral sea.

Then he heard the call from the Great Horn, its
    strident sound-waves blasting
        concentrically forward through the
air to his mechanism on both sides of his
head and at the two sides of his brain
which were his ears, like carved ivory machines that
    ping on precision, plock or chime at the
        right time —
his ears in a way the creators of what they
    hear, or at least

that was another theory of the universe which came
rolling through his opened window unannounced and
unbidden. Never a dull moment!
Lightning-bolts landing everywhere, like
    white chickens from the
        roof of a coop!

2

To grasp for one millisecond a bead of
    genuine light enough to
        ignite every hair follicle for an instant
that lights up the back of any thriving metropolis
casting its lazy silhouette against the night sky —
Oh yes, to hold the truth in its fragile shell like a
twenty-ton grand piano rolling down logs to the
    sea being played on by a suddenly
        undeaf Beethoven able to hear even the
squeek of the birth of a moon in a distant galaxy

as well as the dying words of a spider to its web
or the motherly words of a cricket to her
      babies leaping away.

The theories kept rolling in, they arrived newly
   packaged and unwrapped themselves
     ceremoniously with each breath,
and they were
   truly breathtaking, from the
     first theoretician to the last,
their abstract testimonies somewhat tarnished as they
   slowly vanished into the surrounding
atoms that ebbed and
   flowed in the
     polished varnish of the surface world
      around them.

Nothing left but
voices in the night, entertaining themselves by the
day's last light.

3

Why do these knowledges always elude us, these
   complicated maps of other worlds which
fit down snugly over this one but in
   unexpected extensions and
     unimagined implications, the shape of
 it the actual structure of it, how it
interacts with us or flows out from our own

ignited bodies walking in a nimbus of
    bright blue flame down all the
corridors of our existence, drifting into
one room after another of
    explanation and wisdom or
        boredom and sleep.

Aren't all the dimensions known in our own physiques,
all the juicy mechanisms of our
    thinking machine, each slurp and squeeze of
        organ digesting or alchemizingly transforming
            food or air into nourishment, aren't these
universe pouring out of universe?

I sit on a grassy hill in humid summer in
  lush green Pennsylvania in the late, late
afternoon, gray sky, a light green field before me,
a line of dark trees, sudden rain drops on my
    notebook direct from
        God's mercy —
then go to my car so the drops won't splotch my words
and hear them patter their tiny drumming fingers on the roof —
and close the window and put on the
  air conditioning, since the temperature
    seems to have risen with the rain,
and I prop my notebook against a newly purchased used
    coffee table book on the steering wheel while
Ibn 'Arabi's cosmologies, and Ouspensky's
    complex mathematical explanations
toss through my head,

and universes perfectly mirroring this one but made of
   anti-matter, and
universes of true being of which this one is
   mist coalescing and
     dissolving, out of focus next to that
true universe's clarity,
or the universe in a bubble, a dew drop, a
   raindrop hurtling in sweet
     motion down onto
   the rooftop of my gray Chevy Prizm
facing green fields and trees now
splattered with the

pure rain of time.

4

"It has a god," "It doesn't" —
"There is a god," "There isn't" —

Meanwhile perfect babies are born with perfect
little fists and blue or black eyes,
buoyant things sail through the sky, a leaf
   extends.
Structures continue to build and
   unbuild themselves, of
micro-organisms, of crystals, of
tribal councils of wise old fools on
   tropical islands who
after pondering for a month or two

vote whether or not to move a
   big rock from the lagoon.

"Is there a god, or isn't there?"
stands poised like some beautiful swimmer at the
   top of a golden waterfall whose
     every drop about to
   cascade down with terrific force
is a perfectly formed ovoid sphere
held between invisible fingertips.
A perfect dawn breaks over the scene.
Light filters all the way from the sun
   across ninety-three million miles of darkness
so that one tiny gnat named Halador-Zalagoot can
     bask in it while he
bobs on a leaf.

Otherworldly seas crash against otherworldly
   shores in splendid isolation.
Their diamond beaches glitter in the
     same sun.
Beyond those other worlds, eternity
   washes through infinity like
a transparent wave.

"Is there a god, or isn't there?"
rolls its single cubical die with
     single dots on each side

along a table smooth as ice
in spectacular precincts.

                              7/12-26

POEM ON MY 55th BIRTHDAY

O Lord, when we close our eyes tonight
   where will we be taken? Where will you
take us? Will we

find ourselves on some late night side street
   under pale streetlamp
among killers and kissers, not sure
   which one's a killer and which a kisser?

Will we be happily opening coconuts under shadows of
   palm trees and green cockatoo wingspread
by cerulean seas? For our
transport is certain. We, in sleep, don't

stay long in one place, speeding
among similar time-warp victims helplessly expressed
   elsewhere here,
meeting total strangers or strange
   friends in deep-shadowed hoods and cassocks on
     cold stone floors in
       gloomy corridors or
in fancy formal dress in fancy formal balls in Southern France
dancing the minuet or the mazurka.

Soldiers behind sandbags in bombed-out
cities in the Balkans
must wish they could dream right now,
close their sore eyes and let You

take them where You
   will.

As for me, I'm safely
sitting on my bed. My face feels like a
  crumpled page. The house is still. Others
are all asleep. Cicadas outside
  creak their regular
    creaks. The night is
long, the morning
coming close.

I'm 55 tonight, heading
  toward the Day.

7/30

DEALS

"Take her" he said, trading his most
   oompah djinn with the crazy eyes
   ands swivel hips for
guaranteed territory of dream, priceless
   real estate in the Unseen. Now he can
close his eyes and expect miracles.

"You can have it all," she relented, ceding
a thousand acres of virgin forest
in exchange for one handsome prince
   with lissome physique and a
     good singing voice. *"My days and
nights are now akin to Paradise,"* she
     warbled.

"All right, then, keep it all!" the gin-sloshed
    pirate yelled at top lung
   lashed to the mast, as he
watched his treasure chests slide into an angry sea,
not sure if there was a
   trade in the bargain, as his
men cowered and held onto whatever they could
   on the foaming deck. Only the

black sea had an answer, and the
black sea only roared.

Bargains, exchanges, deals.

Who do we think we are in this most
    merciful of universes? Everything
cohabits, co-writes, co-operates, all of us are
cohorts in the inevitable
    chain of events.

Nothing lasts in stasis. Everything
trembles for joy. It's

all about to disappear anyway.

We sing a warrior's song.

                                                             8/3

TISSUE PAPER

The floor before me, walls and trees
flutter in the Next World's breeze,
waver like thin tissue paper,
elongate in airy vapor.

Everything that's in sun's glow,
including me, has got to go,
fragile substance based on light
slithers away before our sight.

The details of this sheer existence
file away without resistance,
into the darkness of a drawer,
into a silence like a roar

of thunder bouncing off the hills
and every 3-D picture still
shot dissipates its vivid hues
and leaves a trail of valuable clues,

deciphering the very Source
Divine Light transmits with a force
of subtle power in a breeze
through floor and walls, earth and trees.

8/6

THEIR LIPS ARE SINGING

The hat says *"farewell"* to the head
   and continues the journey on its own.

The path says *"adios"* to the earth
   and heads off in a true direction.

Shoes say *"goodbye"* to feet, tap dance on the
   Riviera hoping to hoof it into
     shoe heaven.

The love letter says *"au revoir"* to its sender
   and streaks into the blue sky in search of
     everyone's Beloved.

Everything says *"so long"* to everything else
in this world created to die...
   a long, slow
     "sayonara"...

And then when all 3-D pictures slide into
   sweet repose at last, energy
     drained,
no longer blocking our view,

a Light turns on in a window so deep no
   adequate words can
     express it,

but messengers continue to come
forward from that momentous
   event, carrying their

heads in their hands.

But their lips are singing.

8/9

UNFORESEEN MIRACLES

Someone asked to be shown a miracle
and suddenly a floor took place under him
and four walls and a roof, a window
with clear glass flashed into place, a
    lightbulb with a filament bright enough to
        light up a room electrically
            charged, and outside
grass on a hill friddled back and forth in a
late summer breeze, and somewhere
just out of sight, a cricket the size of a
cricket sang its song, a bird flew by
    pursued by another bird the same size under a
great ball of gases and flames so igneously
hot and violent it would
incinerate a piano and melt down the
    iron inside in a matter of seconds.

He was unimpressed. He wanted something
more along the lines of a bowl with
    unending food appearing in it, or
water to be gushing out of fingertips, or the
    raising of the dead.
The intricate skeletal-work of a leaf was too
    little a thing for him, the air we breathe
too unremarkable, his lungs
taking in air in his chest and the oxygen
going into his blood and the blood circulating through
tiny and less tiny tubes for maybe miles inside him

and throbbing in great jolts through the
atriums and ventricles of his heart which is the
size of a small cabbage and keeps him going up
hill and down dale, up stairs and down
town past department store window displays
just didn't impress him all that much, who wanted

a flame to appear in the air in front of him
or a visit from someone long dead to come in and say,

"Hi, honey, how're ya do'in!

You're a sight for sore eyes!"

8/10

SINK OR SWIM

All ponds on the rise
    ridgeland shrub dotted waterdrop slide
drop by drop added
    landslide around it

crater disappearing water remaining
an impossibility you say
you standing in the middle of the room naked
the way you were born
    not a stitch on
        all smooth sunlit all perfectly formed
as a waterdrop

We also hang from a spout
we also added to the total volume

land gone water stays
suspended in air like a huge globe

we sink or swim

PARADOX LAKE

Tonight I met someone who's going on a Church Retreat
to Paradox Lake.
Wouldn't it be nice if everything were named as
   truthfully?
Calamity Falls. Stiff-Back Camp Ground.
   Treachery Trail.

Or in a more urban setting:
   Crime-Pays-In-The-Shortrun Avenue,
Unsatisfied Desire Shopping Mall,
   Camouflage Clothiers, Digestive Tract Foods,
Rob-You-Blind Department Store,
   We'll-Use-It-And-Lose-It National Bank,
Usurer's Savings and Loan,
   Flames-of-Hell Financing,
When-You-See-The-Bill-You'll-Wish-You-Were-Dead
   General Hospital.

Society's Breakdown Day-Care.
Momentary Oblivion Liquors.
Last-Chance-For-Losers Pawn Shop.
Brainwash U.

Paradox Lake.

8/15

TERRAIN OF THE HEART

The terrain of the heart is a
   rough terrain, with a
silver lake at the top, and shade from the
     heart's root tree.
There golden swans waddle contendedly.
There pollen drifts through the air at an
   alarming rate for those with
     allergies. The pollen soon covers
all available surfaces.
A thin film of golden pollen on everything,
and small light beams that
   follow the flight of birds,
     and distant cries like
  something needing reply, and
the reply comes. A

voice of resonant thunder booms through the
corridors of the heart, then its
   shadow and its shudder, echo upon echo
to our ears, where we
stay alert like
   rabbits suddenly
sitting up.

That voice is God's voice, and that
listening is God's listening. In between
is God's in-between
in the space of the heart.

And slowly someone rises from a puddle of shadow
and assumes erect posture with two arms
   making a circle as if holding a
      disk of light.
God's voice bathes his form in miracles.
That's all that can be said.

And light falls off him in giant
   flakes that drift horizontally
      over the silver lake.
There. Where no shadow is but
shade from the heart's root tree.
Where clear waters babble.

Where turmoil lays down its head
and gives itself up for lost.

Where anger like a knotted rope
finally falls from the ceiling
   into the lake.

Where bewilderment makes its way, baffled, through the
   intense brightness as if
      blinded by light.

Where love washes its face there
   over and over in the

waters of the silver lake.

8/18

A TRILLION THINGS

A trillion things are waiting for attention
   under the early morning blanket of
      starry skies, troops of
         light are lining up on the horizon,
banging each other with great white wings
trying to get in order before the
   dawn-light hits them, and

heat insects, wallowing in humidity like
Russians in mud baths at a country spa,
make their hypnotic electronic music in
     spatial avenues, on trees, under bushes,
        getting the acoustics just right,

and as the day comes these
trillion things, a bird with a broken wing,
   afraid under a branch for
     cats and hawks,
a little girl's broken bicycle, she waiting to
  wake up and exact the payment of
   last night's promise from her dad,
irritable world leaders who only want
sex and hot dinners, waiting the day when they
file into a stuffy room to talk about
where millions of helpless, shell-shocked
    citizens under their paternal
  care will be forced to live, if they
      live at all,

and each situation is as tender as a fresh wound
waiting for some cooling cream to be applied,
and the cooling cream is that mysterious mixture of
Grace and piquant stinging that comes
   directly from God, it may not be
a silly sweetness that prompts everyone to
     burst into song, it may be
a thousand little stitches crisscrossed and
        pinching, but the

clear-eyed may cry out in joy at that
   sudden administering, and the
dying may roll their eyes in its direction as if it were
     light coming down a stairs,

and the leaper to his death may suddenly see
   the golden cord of it
     to grab onto, and the
swimmer may see the topaz rocks of the
opposite shore suddenly heave into view,
and the cricket may see the object of his
   quest dangling behind a
     chewable leaf,

and the trillion things awaiting God's attention,
stars behind dust-clusters and the
original intention, even hidden to me, of this
   poem, all hope for a quick
turning of His attention from all the
    other trillion things

to beam a Divine Glance like a
trillion silver birds flying forward
to write comprehensible phrases in our hearts
with their
spectacularly visible wings.

                                                        8/19

TRAIN WRECK REVERSED

Time and space backtrack from the train wreck,
cars magnificently uncrumple, a deafening roar sucks
   back into the balmy silence of
     gnats and bird chirps in the
        precise moment preceding it,
a little black girl flies backwards through the air and
lands happily singing to herself
   by the side of the tracks,
people fly back unbloodying themselves,
lacerations smooth over and
torn limbs join torsos and return to normal,

some of the passengers
come remarkably back to life in the
   midst of an animated conversation, passenger cars
flip back onto tracks and are
coupled in their proper order, babies slip
miraculously back into cuddling arms,
passengers slip noisily back into their seats
   through the jagged metallic
     rip that closes now with the
   reversed sound of its ripping,
passengers pop back behind books, adjust
glasses, pick noses or
curl sideways on their seats with their
heads resting on greasy backpacks,

the horror on the engineer's face returns to the placid

concentration he's had for exactly
  an hour and twelve minutes, he
    sips his coffee and glances sideways at a
gauge,
gigantic bursts of flame go
back into the pinpoints of their sources like
genies zooming back into metallic bottles and
    pulling their corks in behind them,
angels surround the moving train
in their usual harmonious order, spectacular with
thought and gorgeous with
molecular obedience, moving through the air like
      raindrops falling from a cloud,

the critical moment hasn't come, history hasn't been
transformed, the flash of news remains
hidden in the future, newspaper reporters'
ears have yet to be bombarded with descriptions of
    disaster,
God's pre-eternal decree hasn't yet
revealed itself through the mysterious dimensions of
our bodies,

the nine-fifteen chugs along in the nimbus of
  its usual sense of
immortality, past pine trees and

farm houses,
accelerating slightly
as it heaves round the unforeseeable
    bend.

8/21

THE LAND OF DREAMS

The land of dreams fits in a nutshell,
   sits in a thimble, sinks in a
     soap bubble, like the
questioning face of an ultra-bright
eight-year-old
the dream beams its light through us until we
surface, then flaps home empty-handed like a
vulture away from well-guarded meat.

One of the two worlds on either side is real,
   undergoes whimsical transformation, leaps from
tragedy to comedy in a matter of seconds,
wears a giraffe head to dinner, has the world's biggest
ocean liner sink among icebergs, wages war in
   feathered capes and armaments of
     glass and blue powder, swims
singlehandedly across the Hellespont, sings at the

top of its lungs until all the goblets break.

One of the two worlds on either side of the glass
has us in it, or very reasonable
   facsimiles, who come to life inside the
stomach of another, emerge into fully
   quadrupedaled life, then bi-pedaled,
     goes off to China in the Peace Corps, or
       Borneo with plastic tarpaulin,

gets old and nostalgic and finally
closes eyes and nostrils and lets fingers and
    toes unclench and our pure original spirit
lifts out of it like fresh-cut roses
        lifted by a lover from a box, and our spirit
drifts to its first region, counting its
    blessings and
        glad to be going home —

in one of the two worlds all this happens,
in one of the two worlds facing each other through a
    two-way glass, but each side
happily distorting the 3-D pictures in their own way,
one side seemingly photo-realistic but
    highly exaggerated and generally erroneous,
the other side
surreally juxtaposed but oddly reasonable, giving
    mysterious messages of deepest
        import that may
point the way to
        ultimate perfection.

The Land of Dreams, the Land of Reality,
pointillistically dotted through each others' territories,

drawing us forward with their
    special enticements

until we are one.

8/24

A HUNDRED LITTLE 3D PICTURES * 271

3-D PICTURES FOR SALE

The shop at the corner of
Fabrication Boulevard and Imagination Avenue
was fresh out of forms to
   excite the mind.
The smiling merchant of 3-D pictures behind the counter
  had on his black skullcap
    and his lips fluttered like the
wings of a happy hummingbird.

He was an angelic agent on a
televangelistic errand to earth:
to supply the pictures. But he'd
   momentarily run out.

The afternoon sun would have
   shone down on a green
     hillside,
a distant cow in a distant field
   would have chewed her endless cud,
but the merchant had
momentarily run out of every picture
   imaginable, so these
things didn't happen. The boastful

gnat didn't skim above the mirror
surface of a glassy pond, the shy,
    tow-headed, freckle-faced
   farm boy didn't ever-so-slowly take the

    milky white hand of the
plump, blond farm girl for the first time —

as the merchant grinned and fluttered his silent lips
war didn't grind to its
   ultimate conclusions, maimed and
     dead didn't disport themselves
       everywhere,
airplanes didn't fall out of bright blue skies
  into deep dark ravines,
Mrs. Lutwiler didn't turn in lacy waltz time
   under the stiff arm of
the Count Luchasse de Stromberg,

and the smiling merchant scratched his
  head under his black skullcap,
his great gossamer wings opened and
   shut slowly, majestic in their
deliberation, something one could

describe metaphorically for
a billion years and never quite catch

the sense of grandeur, and the second sense of
   echoing blessedness such a

stunningly detailed description might yield.

                                                             8/30

PERMISSION FOR SILENCE

The brave wanderer pushed back his hood
  and his face was a passing cloud.

He was at the crest of the peak.

He was riding the dark red beast.
The beast rose up on its hind legs of
  iron metropolis drawbridge catatonic
windswept emptiness and yowled

  forward across the centuries into oblivion's back pocket
  and the wanderer stood up in his stirrups and also
  yowled and all the birds leaned forward on their
  branches and sang the song of redemption from
  Death Without Consciousness

  and it was a canyon of light that opened up in the
  air and it was filled with crisscrossed
  voices snapping like banners and going off like
  flares everywhere

  but the wanderer who had his road tattooed on his
  back by the divine pulse
  stood up in his stirrups and looked with his
  full eyes into the next era, the
    world to come, transition into space, and he

  turned the beast for a moment from the summit

and went down into the gorge with its
livid red ravines, its tongues of flame, its
rifts of eyes watching the passing figure
and blinking, into the
   smoke, disappearing deep down in
like someone in quicksand, this

peculiar narrative also sinking, this
frosting out of EdgarAllen Poe, this
shriek held in midair, this
cry like a fireball lobbed into the night and
passing slow.

This permission for silence.

9/2

CONTENTMENT'S GARDEN

The grass is variable, the Black-eyed Susans getting
   scrawny, on the row-house balcony next to me
a baseball announcer growls out his commentary,
a cricket behind the garbage cans is
   rehearsing its genealogy at top voice, or
     calling a friend, or just
       singing for pleasure,

annoyed by the radio, annoyed most intensely by the
baseball commentary and crowd-roar that crashes through what was
going to be a poem about my perfect garden and my
perfect contentment in it (in spite of distant dog-yap and
   echo of complaining neighbors), a few moments ago
before the neighbor switched the radio on again after a
     brief respite, I was sitting in my little

backyard eating lunch looking up at my mimosa tree,
its graceful lattice-like fronds making a lovely canopy,
some of the fronds crossing over each other to make an
   almost moiré crisscross pattern,

and I thought of those sepia tintypes of
   Robert Lewis Stevenson in Hawaii on his
     porch with Polynesian ladies with long black
hair, and how he didn't have
anything on me, in my garden contentment,

and Henri Rousseau with his jungly paintings of

fantasy savagery under
      radar-like moonlight and how I
didn't need to imagine blue-feathered
cranes crossing a white sky, or
   lyre-birds displaying the geysering "S's" of their
      tail plumage, my little

split-bamboo fenced garden in which I'd planted some
grocery store petunias and a pampered baby maple tree
was perfect, I sat in a green cloud, I
   floated over the silver lagoon of my thoughts, I
could gaze happily into the
   quiet volcano of my heart, the
      human heart in general, watch

China shake its fists at the world, or
Havana sit back in the baking sun and sigh,
watch tiny amoebas make friends and devour
   enemies in transparent bloodstreams,
hear the sounds of a distant coming-to-birth of
ecstatic inspiration, or watch the
elegant death of a man of God whose mouth makes
  phrases of golden light as he
    sinks into heaven's foam,

all from this unpainted wooden garden chair I
salvaged from our back alley on rubbish day,
from this postage-stamp sized portion of
   Paradise with its
      bird-tweets and cricket screech,

even its baseball games and brake screech,

as I close my eyes for a moment to formulate these
lines and see I am watching a vague green
   planet of light that lies just
      inside us, place of
wonders, place of
  passing sights, port of
ultimate nothingness before the

dimensionless

distinct *somethingness* of the

Face of God.

9/3

A HUNDRED LITTLE 3D PICTURES

1

A thousand little 3D pictures, a
   billion, each postage-stamp sized or
less, triangular, circular,

they spill into the universe like coins from a
   winning slot machine, they skim through the
air to us like a herd of excited flying squirrels, they assemble and
reassemble without glue or guile,
they sail through the air with the greatest of ease
and float into place like dirigibles
honing in for a landing.

Their Captain eases them in. He knows the score.
Nothing is omitted or detained from their
   reaching their goal. They are our world.

If a bug waltzes by, he's it.
If a fire breaks out, it's it.
If we all go home, that's it.

Everything accomplished.

2

One: The nose on baby Snookums.

Two: The ancient Bridge at Karnak.
Three: Two zebras mating.
Four: Yellow umbrellas in high wind.
Five: but the list is endless. Covers
   all the eras, every peak and valley of
     human achievement, every instance of
divine intervention, false starts and
   abrupt stops, faulty machinery, smooth-running digital
twelve-dimensional universal tail-display of forms congenial or
monstrous such as this table before me piled with books
not transforming into ravenous dragon eating my leg
although it could both in this
poem and in reality although it would be
   going against the norm to
     such a degree as to be
improbable. That's the way these things

operate, according to divine laws set down as
meticulously for the petals of
   chrysanthemum as for
     infant lips or dragonfly's
       eyeballs.

3

All the worlds are precious and come
   surging from the deeps.

O, saintly ones arranged in heavenly levels
before saintly ones. Angelic spans of light

   across a vast horizon!

Names tumbling forward out of amethyst lips.

We watch them sail through the air.

Sometimes they stand for something and we
   see that something and
     remember the name.

What rim of continent, what
  surf of ocean, what
    stretch of beach as far as the
      eye can see
upon which man's life depends?

The last word said on lips as the
  body's lowered down
    geological level by geological

level to be laid to rest somewhere in the
Jurassic era, or back even

farther, our constituent atoms sucking
backwards into the Big Bang, humming that

catchy
interplanetary tune!

                                           9/7-9

BLUE IS AN EXCELLENT COLOR FOR SKY

Blue is a color excellent for sky.

Earth covers us all at last.

Mental telepathy takes place in a flash.

We are suddenly placing a healing
hand on a throbbing pain
   and the other person is healed. No

flags waved in the breeze alerted us to the need,
only God's good pleasure put one and one
   together to make: One.

Rainbows in curved air, straight rainbow
   particles arching over splendor.

Above them: Angelic hoedown.
Below them: Angelic fiesta.

Basically it's all creatures of light

and we're enjoined to

enjoy it.

                                                    9/11

AIR

The one I love's not behind a cloud
      or hidden in the air.
The one I love leaves traces of her presence
      everywhere.

A waterfall opens up over rocks, a
      butterfly opens its wings —
my beloved's reflection has just left the
      mirror provided by "things."

There's no space between us, actually, I
      feel her breath.
But I will not know how close we are
      until my death.

If I look for her face I will see my own,
      if I look in my heart, she's there.
Sometimes I wander through the streets
      in dumb despair.

Why has she left me here like a fool,
      bouncing like a ball?
Does she not think of me, does she not really
      care at all?

If I go into wood, I find her. If I
      go into air, she's there.
If I go into water, I hear her gentle
      laughter appear.

Her voice holds me even more strongly than
    her eyes.
Though her eyes gaze with an intense seeing
    that knows no size.

The melody of her words and voice are what
    leads me on.
Even when the world is silent as a feather
    I hear her song.

She's not distant, she's told me. Not
    visible, she's near.
I call out her name, and without any
    ostentation, she's here.

As any normal lover would, I want to
    hold her in my arms.
No one would blame me for this if they only
    knew her charms.

No one would wonder why I stand so long
    in a dangerous place
just for the feel of her breath or one
    glimpse of her face.

I can't go on with mere reports, or mere
    echoes of her name.
If I can't speak my love sincerely, I'm just a
    flickering flame.

Let me go from the clutches of everyone and
	everything but her.
Let the whole world transform its vision
	into an endless blur.

She calls me through corridors and hallways,
	she stands in a door.
I'm going to where she is, as I did
	before.

What are birth and death to me now, what are
	Paradise or Hell
without being with my beloved, and being
	able to tell?

O bring me a drink of water, and let me wet my
	lips.
Let me look down onto the reflection
	as I take my sips.

I don't want to see my own face, or
	anything of me.
I want my beloved to be the only
	thing I see.

Everywhere my eye falls, from earth to
	sky,
let me only see her face, then
	let me die.

9/11

INDEX

A Bizarre Episode Concerning Stigmata   85
A Hundred Little 3D Pictures   279
A Hundred People in a Room   174
A Place for the Night   244
A Trillion Things   265
A Very Short Poem   236
Afraid of Mortality   59
Ah, That Unseizeable Moment   152
Air   283
Alchemical Jewels   106
All the Books I Need   35
Ancient Ziggurat   205
Angels   64
Are We Hugged by Angels?   157
At Sea   212
Author's Introduction   10
Aw, Go to Sleep   225
Bad Stanzas   209
Between a Promise and a Taunt   29
Blue Scarf of Lights   127
Blue is an Excellent Color for Sky   282
Bookstore Coffee Shop   94
Borealis Sky   80
Contentment's Garden   276
Continuum   141
Cosmic Paradox   229
Deals   254
Death Bed   52
Death and Language   100

Doorknob   232
Eight Short Life Stories   237
Elaborations/Simplifications   74
Every Poet is Foolish   149
Everyone at the Mall   193
Fist   14
Folk Poems   131
Giant Dog   27
Glass Skull   43
God's Observation Window   129
History Lesson   154
How Does Reality Come Through to Us?   25
If You Worship a Goat's Head   168
I'm Awakened by Something   116
Leaves   58
New Maple Tree   39
New Onset Atrial Fibrillation   87
New York, New York   21
Ocean City, New Jersey   71
Palace in the Treetops   204
Panga   47
Paradox Lake   262
Parallel Rose   33
Permission for Silence   274
Poem Written During the Interview by Charlie Rose
    of Robert McNamara April 19, 1995 in Which McNamara
    States That the Vietnam War Was Wrong   188
Poem Written Out in the Coffee Bar   145
Poem on my 55th Birthday   252
Preparations for Sleep   190
Rawhide Figure   239

Saints Everywhere   41
Seven Short Fables   234
Shake the Box   222
Silver Water from a Spout   242
Sink or Swim   261
Six Couplets   107
Sleep and Waking   82
Some Spiritual Secrets   84
Stone   18
Sweet Cosmologies   246
Taking Shape   31
Terrain of the Heart   263
The Ballad of Rosalee   182
The Conference of the Dead   109
The Excavation   136
The Field is a Fuzzy Conglomeration   13
The Imager   118
The Journey   76
The Joy of Composition   15
The Land of Dreams   270
The Little 3D Picture of Death   23
The Man with One Eye   194
The Mummy   16
The Naked Fishermen of Tinderzee   171
The Oceans of Love   197
The Process   144
The Sentence   123
The Slow Wingbeat of Butterflies   184
The Sweet Grief of Loss   50
Theft of a Coat   177
Their Lips are Singing   257

These Faces of Ours   163
3D Pictures for Sale   272
Tissue Paper   256
Top of the World, Bottom of the World   78
Train Wreck Reversed   268
Twentieth Century Justice   45
Unforeseen Miracles   259
Various Meetings with the Self   166
Various Poems I Wanted to Write   62
Wall of the Elements   19
When I Pray   160
Written During a Rainstorm   159

ABOUT THE AUTHOR

Born in 1940 in Oakland, California, Daniel Abdal-Hayy Moore had his first book of poems, *Dawn Visions*, published by Lawrence Ferlinghetti of City Lights Books, San Francisco, in 1964, and the second in 1972, *Burnt Heart/Ode to the War Dead*. He created and directed *The Floating Lotus Magic Opera Company* in Berkeley, California in the late 60s, and presented two major productions, *The Walls Are Running Blood*, and *Bliss Apocalypse*. He became a Sufi Muslim in 1970, performed the Hajj in 1972, and lived and traveled throughout Morocco, Spain, Algeria and Nigeria, landing in California and publishing *The Desert is the Only Way Out*, and *Chronicles of Akhira* in the early 80s (Zilzal Press). Residing in Philadelphia since 1990, in 1996 he published *The Ramadan Sonnets* (Jusoor/City Lights), and in 2002, *The Blind Beekeeper* (Jusoor/Syracuse University Press). He has been the major editor for a number of works, including *The Burdah* of Shaykh Busiri, translated by Hamza Yusuf, and the poetry of Palestinian poet, Mahmoud Darwish, translated by Munir Akash. He is also widely published on the worldwide web: *The American Muslim, DeenPort*, and his own website and poetry blog, among others: *www.danielmoorepoetry.com, www.ecstaticxchange.wordpress.com*. He has been poetry editor for *Seasons Journal, Islamica Magazine*, a 2010 translation by Munir Akash of *State of Siege*, by Mahmoud Darwish (Syracuse University Press), and *The Prayer of the Oppressed*, by Imam Muhammad Nasir al-Dar'i, translated by Hamza Yusuf. In 2011 and 2012 he was a winner of the Nazim Hikmet Prize for Poetry. *The Ecstatic Exchange Series* is bringing out the extensive body of his works of poetry (a complete list of published works on page 2).

POETIC WORKS by Daniel Abdal-Hayy Moore
Published and Unpublished

Dawn Visions (published by City Lights, 1964)
Burnt Heart/Ode to the War Dead (published by City Lights, 1972)
This Body of Black Light Gone Through the Diamond (printed by Fred Stone, Cambridge, Mass, 1965)
On The Streets at Night Alone (1965?)
All Hail the Surgical Lamp (1967)
States of Amazement (1970)

Abdallah Jones and the Disappearing-Dust Caper (published by The Ecstatic Exchange/Crescent Series, 2006)
'Ala ud-Deen and the Magic Lamp (published by The Ecstatic Exchange, 2011)
The Chronicles of Akhira (1981) (published by Zilzal Press with Typoglyphs by Karl Kempton, 1986; published in Sparrow on the Prophet's Tomb by The Ecstatic Exchange, 2009)
Mouloud (1984) (A Zilzal Press chapbook, 1995; published in Sparrow on the Prophet's Tomb by The Ecstatic Exchange, 2009)
Man is the Crown of Creation (1984)
The Look of the Lion (The Parabolas of Sight) (1984)
The Desert is the Only Way Out (completed 4/21/84) (Zilzal Press chapbook, 1985)
Atomic Dance (1984) (am here books, 1988)
Outlandish Tales (1984)
Awake as Never Before (12/26/84) (Zilzal Press chapbook, 1993)
Glorious Intervals (1/1/85) (Zilzal Press chapbook, ?)
Long Days on Earth/Book I (1/28 – 8/30/85)
Long Days on Earth/Book II (Hayy Ibn Yaqzan)
Long Days on Earth/Book III (1/22/86)
Long Days on Earth/Book IV (1986)
The Ramadan Sonnets (Long Days on Earth/Book V) (5/9 – 6/11/86) (published by Jusoor/City Lights Books, 1996) (republished as Ramadan Sonnets by The Ecstatic Exchange, 2005)
Long Days on Earth/Book VI (6-8/30/86)
Holograms (9/4/86 – 3/26/87)
History of the World (The Epic of Man's Survival) (4/7 – 6/18/87)
Exploratory Odes (6/25 – 10/18/87)

The Man at the End of the World (11/11 – 12/10/87)
The Perfect Orchestra (3/30 – 7/25/88)(published by The Ecstatic Exchange, 2009)
Fed from Underground Springs (7/30 – 11/23/88)
Ideas of the Heart (11/27/88 – 5/5/89)
New Poems (scattered poems, out of series, from 3/24 – 8/9/89)
Facing Mecca (5/16 – 11/11/89)
A Maddening Disregard for the Passage of Time (11/17/89 – 5/20/90) (published by The Ecstatic Exchange, 2009)
The Heart Falls in Love with Visions of Perfection (6/15/90 – 6/2/91)
Like When You Wave at a Train and the Train Hoots Back at You (Farid's Book) (6/11 – 7/26/91) (published by The Ecstatic Exchange, 2008)
Orpheus Meets Morpheus (8/1/91– 3/14/92)
The Puzzle (3/21/92 – 8/17/93)(published by The Ecstatic Exchange, 2011)
The Greater Vehicle (10/17/93 – 4/30/94)
A Hundred Little 3-D Pictures (5/14/94 – 9/11/95)(published by The Ecstatic Exchange, 2013)
The Angel Broadcast (9/29 – 12/17/95)
Mecca/Medina Time-Warp (12/19/95 – 1/6/96) (published as a Zilzal Press chapbook, 1996)(published in Sparrow on the Prophet's Tomb, 2009)
Miracle Songs for the Millennium (1/20 – 10/16/96)
The Blind Beekeeper (11/15/96 – 5/30/97) (published 2002 by Jusoor/Syracuse University Press)
Chants for the Beauty Feast (6/3 – 10/28/97)(published by The Ecstatic Exchange, 2011
You Open a Door and it's a Starry Night (10/29/97 – 5/23/98) (published by The Ecstatic Exchange, 2009)
Salt Prayers (5/29 – 10/24/98) (published by The Ecstatic Exchange, 2005)
Some (10/25/98 – 4/25/99)
Flight to Egypt (5/1 – 5/16/99)
I Imagine a Lion (5/21 – 11/15/99) (published by The Ecstatic Exchange, 2006)
Millennial Prognostications (11/25/99 – 2/2/2000) (published by the Ecstatic Exchange, 2009)
Shaking the Quicksilver Pool (2/4 – 10/8/2000) (published by The Ecstatic Exchange, 2009)
Blood Songs (10/9/2000 – 4/3/2001)(Published by The Ecstatic Exchange, 2012)
The Music Space (4/10 – 9/16/2001) (published by The Ecstatic Exchange, 2007)

Where Death Goes (9/20/2001 – 5/1/2002) (published by The Ecstatic Exchange, 2009)

The Flame of Transformation Turns to Light (99 Ghazals Written in English) (5/14 – 8/21/2002) (published by The Ecstatic Exchange, 2007)

Through Rose-Colored Glasses (7/22/2002 – 1/15/2003) (published by The Ecstatic Exchange, 2007)

Psalms for the Broken-Hearted (1/22 – 5/25/2003) (published by The Ecstatic Exchange, 2006)

Hoopoe's Argument (5/27 – 9/18/03)

Love is a Letter Burning in a High Wind (9/21 – 11/6/2003) (published by The Ecstatic Exchange, 2006)

Laughing Buddha/Weeping Sufi (11/7/2003 – 1/10/2004) (published by The Ecstatic Exchange, 2005)

Mars and Beyond (1/20 – 3/29/2004) (published by The Ecstatic Exchange, 2005)

Underwater Galaxies (4/5 – 7/21/2004) (published by The Ecstatic Exchange, 2007)

Cooked Oranges (7/23/2004 – 1/24/2005 (published by The Ecstatic Exchange, 2007)

Holiday from the Perfect Crime (1/25 – 6/11/2005)(published by The Ecstatic Exchange, 2011)

Stories Too Fiery to Sing Too Watery to Whisper (6/13 – 10/24/2005)

Coattails of the Saint (10/26/2005 – 5/10/2006) (published by The Ecstatic Exchange, 2006)

In the Realm of Neither (5/14/2006 – 11/12/06) (published by The Ecstatic Exchange, 2008)

Invention of the Wheel (11/13/06 – 6/10/07)(published by The Ecstatic Exchange, 2010)

The Sound of Geese Over the House (6/15 – 11/4/07)

The Fire Eater's Lunchbreak (11/11/07 – 5/19/2008) (published by The Ecstatic Exchange, 2008)

Sparks Off the Main Strike (5/24/2008 – 1/10/2009)(published by The Ecstatic Exchange, 2010)

Stretched Out on Amethysts (1/13 – 9/17/2009)(published by The Ecstatic Exchange, 2010)

The Throne Perpendicular to All that is Horizontal (9/18/09 – 1/25/10)

In Constant Incandescence (2/10 – 8/13/10) (published by The Ecstatic Exchange, 2011)

The Caged Bear Spies the Angel (8/30/10 – 3/6/11)(published by The Ecstatic Exchange, 2010)
This Light Slants Upward (3/7 – 10/13/11)
Ramadan is Burnished Sunlight (part of This Light Slants Upward, published separately by The Ecstatic Exchange, 2011)
The Match That Becomes a Conflagration (10/14/11 – 5/9/12)
Down at the Deep End (5/10 – 8/3/12) (published by The Ecstatic Exchange, 2012)
Next Life (8/9/12 – 2/12/13) (published by The Ecstatic Exchange, 2013)
The Soul's Home (2/13/13 –)

www.ingramcontent.com/pod-product-compliance
Lightning Source LLC
Chambersburg PA
CBHW022053160426
43198CB00008B/211